HOW TO BUY
U.S. REAL ESTATE
WITH THE PERSONAL
PROPERTY PURCHASE
SYSTEM

HOW TO BUY U.S. REAL ESTATE WITH THE PERSONAL PROPERTY PURCHASE SYSTEM

A CANADIAN GUIDE

by KIMBERLEY MARR

WILEY

John Wiley & Sons Canada, Ltd.

RE/MAX® is a registered service mark of RE/MAX International and ABR® is a registered trademark of the Real Estate Buyer's Agent Council (REBAC®), which is a wholly owned subsidiary of the National Association of REALTORS®.

Care has been taken to trace ownership of copyright material contained in this book. The publisher will gladly receive any information that will enable them to rectify any reference or credit line in subsequent editions.

Wiley publishes in a variety of print and electronic formats and by print-on-demand. Some material included with standard print versions of this book may not be included in e-books or in print-on-demand. If this book refers to media such as a CD or DVD that is not included in the version you purchased, you may download this material at http://booksupport.wiley. com. For more information about Wiley products, visit www.wiley.com.

Charts and some information repurposed for this book appeared in *Your First Home: A Buyer's Kit - For Condos and Houses!* (Self-Counsel Press, 2012).

Library and Archives Canada Cataloguing in Publication Data
Marr, Kimberley, 1964-
    How to buy U.S. real estate with the personal property purchase system : a Canadian guide / Kimberley Marr.

Includes index.
Issued also in electronic formats.
ISBN 978-1-118-29681-3

    1. House buying—United States.   2. Home ownership—United States.
3. Investments, Canadian—United States.   4. Real estate investment—United States.   I. Title.

HD255.M37 2012   333.33'830973   C2011-908111-3

ePDF: 978-1-118-30017-6; Mobi: 978-1-118-30022-0; ePub: 978-1-118-30024-4

Production Credits
Cover design: Adrian So
Typesetting: Thomson Digital
Cover image: Thinkstock
Author photo: Scott Cook, Scott Cook Photography
Printer: Dickinson Press

Editorial Credits
Executive editor: Don Loney
Managing editor: Alison Maclean
Production editor: Jeremy Hanson-Finger

John Wiley & Sons Canada, Ltd.
6045 Freemont Blvd.
Mississauga, Ontario
L5R 4J3

Printed in U.S.A.

1 2 3 4 5 DP 16 15 14 13 12

*To my amazing Mom & Dad, with all my love
and gratitude. You always encouraged me to follow my dreams.*

*To my dear friend Dollina, who passed away during
the time I wrote this book. Your courage, grace, and optimistic outlook
are unforgettable. I will miss you.*

A NOTE TO THE READER

CONTENTS

Contents

FOREWORD

Over the past five years, residential property prices in the United States have fallen significantly—in some places by as much as 50 per cent. America is on sale, and the value one can realize by investing in U.S. real estate, compared to other countries around the world, is extraordinary. Whether purchasing a property for personal use or as an investment, selection has never been better and interest rates are at an all-time low.

For the enthusiastic but inexperienced buyer, the process of purchasing property outside of one's country of residence can seem daunting and complicated. I'm happy to say that at long last we have an excellent guide that will help both the novice and experienced buyer. It explains the buying process clearly and concisely in language that is easy to understand.

How to Buy U.S. Real Estate points out the potential pitfalls one should avoid, the cautions one should take, and the incredible opportunity at the doorstep of Canadians. As you reflect on what your next investment will be—seeking a place in the sun or thinking ahead to a permanent vacation or retirement property that you can call your own—this information-packed guide will provide you with deep insight to help you make your purchase decision a wise one.

Personally, over the past seven years, I have purchased two properties in the United States and I wish I could have had this book at my disposal. Even though I am an expert in the real estate industry, I faced many complicated issues that took time and effort to solve. Information is everything, and had this book been available it would have made my experience so much easier.

I made these investments because I believe in the value of real estate and I especially believe in the unique opportunity that exists *right now* in the United States. My decisions were based on value, investment, future retirement, and the opportunity for long-term appreciation. Put the Personal Property Purchase System to work for you; it will provide you with invaluable information and help you make the decision that is right for your personal or investment strategy. Enjoy the book—I certainly did.

Pamela Alexander,
CEO RE/MAX® Integra Corporation

CHAPTER 1

The Opportunity

Why Do You Want to Buy U.S. Real Estate?

Rob, Cathy, and their son Andrew were carpooling with Terry and her son Michael to the boys' playoff hockey game at the Icedome in north Toronto. The boys—both forwards on the Blackhawks team—were busy in the backseat reviewing, in between Game Boy victories, the break-out strategies their hockey team had practiced the previous evening. The morning was frosty, and the parents were talking about the long, cold winter, the fact that the playoffs marked the end of another busy hockey season, and how they were looking forward to the warmer spring weather that was fast approaching.

This time of year was especially busy for Terry, a real estate broker, and Rob and Cathy were getting used to the nonstop calls Terry was taking on her cell phone. They didn't want to appear nosy, but their curiosity was piqued as they overheard Terry speaking about the state of the housing market in the U.S., foreclosures, mortgages—and warm weather.

Cathy finally chirped up and said that her next-door neighbour and a colleague at work just purchased vacation property in the U.S. Terry nodded and told her, "During this last year, a number of Canadians and associates have purchased real estate in the U.S. And this trend is on the rise."

Rob said he was not surprised to hear this—so far, two of his colleagues had purchased property in Florida that winter. Both felt they got a great deal on their properties, as prices in the areas they purchased had declined more than 50 per cent compared with a few years ago and the Canadian dollar was close to parity.

Cathy echoed Rob's thoughts: "Rob and I have talked about how nice it would be to buy a property somewhere warm to escape these cold winters, and to have it for retirement. From what we're hearing and reading, we don't know if we will ever again get such a great opportunity to buy real estate in the Sunbelt, what with prices this affordable compared to just a few years ago, our loonie this high, and interest rates this attractive. It seems like now is the time to really think this through."

Terry responded, "I have read statistics that tell us that Canadians were one of the larger groups of foreign buyers of U.S. real estate in 2011. Unfortunately, many Canadians don't understand all the factors involved in buying in another country; some aspects of the process of looking for, and making an offer on a property may be similar to how it works in Canada, but the U.S. is a different country, with different tax, estate, and other rules and laws.

"Consideration also needs to be given to health care, as well as insurance issues. And there are several important money-saving and asset-protection strategies that should be considered and incorporated into a U.S. purchase plan. It is not as easy as just looking online at a few properties or going to a seminar where properties are showcased and buying one," continued Terry.

"So what type of questions are Canadian buyers typically asking?" inquired Rob.

"Essentially, while there is a great deal of interest and excitement about the prospect of purchasing a U.S. property, there is also fear of the unknown, and most questions revolve around how to start," replied Terry.

"That's exactly how I feel," Cathy responded. "While it sounds fantastic, we really don't know who to contact or how we should go about obtaining information. I read and hear about other Canadians purchasing real estate in Florida and other parts of the U.S., but I'm unsure of how to proceed. We're trying to balance the need to act with the realization that this would be a big investment—and that it took years to manage and save our money, and pay off the mortgage on our house. We need direction."

Terry replied, "I have created a buyer's program that provides information and resources for Canadian buyers on many factors they should understand before purchasing U.S. real estate. There are important rules and compliance tasks that Canadians need to be aware of if they own property and spend time in the U.S. A Canadian buyer of U.S. property should consult with cross-border financial and legal professionals to ensure they under-stand and structure the transaction appropriate to their individual needs and situation. The program outlines appropriate tools and resources and, through the network, Canadians can access cross-border mortgage professionals, as well as U.S. real estate brokers, to assist them in the process."

Terry's phone rang again and she excused herself.

"Cathy, if it's all right with Terry, maybe now is the time to get more information from her on how we could buy a Florida home. She may be able to give us the answers to some of our questions—house or condo? On the ocean or a lake? Imagine being able to play a few rounds of golf each month, and go boating and fishing!" said an excited Rob.

"What would we do with the house when we weren't there? Would we rent it out, and if so, to whom?" asked Cathy.

"Hey, Mom, are you and Dad buying a house in Florida?" asked Andrew. The conversation has caught the boy's attention.

"Just ask my mom about real estate," said Michael, rolling his eyes.

Rob laughed. "Yes, we can see how busy your mother is. Do you get to visit the sunny south with your mom?"

"Sometimes. It sure is a lot warmer there in the middle of winter. I usually go during Christmas break, March break, or at Easter."

"Do you like it? Is it cool?" asked Andrew.

"Yes, it's fun. I get to see my grandma and grandpa, and sometimes my cousins. We all go together," said Michael.

"Sounds like a great time," replied Cathy.

Rob pulled the van into the arena parking lot just as Terry finished her phone call. As Rob was pulling out the equipment bags, Andrew piped up, "Hey, Mom, can we go with Michael and Terry and their family on a trip to Florida? I remember the last time we went—it was so much fun."

"Boys, it's time to focus on your game. We win and we advance. Remember the skills your coach had you work on this week. We'll talk about Florida later," said Cathy. She leaned over and whispered to Terry, "I have a few real estate questions—can we chat after the game?"

The boys gathered up their hockey bags and skates. The parents grabbed their blankets and cushions, and off they went—the boys to the dressing room and the parents to find seats to watch and cheer them on. Playoff hockey at the boys' level was exciting; the boys were skilled, highly competitive, and old enough to understand the importance of teamwork, strategy, and a game plan—aspects not unlike buying a U.S. property. The key words are "game plan" and "strategy."

The boys played hard and doubled their opponents 6–3. Michael and Andrew had two assists each. As was customary during playoffs, many of the parents gathered for dinner after the game.

"Meet at the restaurant in 15 minutes," confirmed Jay and Helen.

"Sounds great. See you there," responded Rob.

The boys loaded their equipment into the van and Rob, Cathy, and Terry were on their way. "Way to go boys—one step closer to the championship," said Terry.

"Thanks! Hey, Mom, is Andrew coming with us on our next trip to Florida?" asked Michael.

"Boy, that didn't take long, did it?" laughed Terry. "We'll talk about it."

Cathy and Rob glanced at each other and smiled. Cathy added, "When convenient, we would really like to find out more about the buying a property in Florida."

"I would be delighted to share the buyer's program with you. Let's set up an appointment to go through your questions and thoughts and see if this is a route you would like to explore," replied Terry.

"Brrrr, somehow this cold really goes through me," said Cathy, shuddering. "It sure would be nice to escape this weather for a little while every year."

They arrived at the restaurant, and Andrew ran ahead to find the team. "Hey, everyone," he announced, "my parents are buying a house in Florida, and you are all invited."

All eyes turned toward Rob and Cathy, who had by now caught up. "Oh, wow! How lucky are you?" said one of the parents.

"Where in Florida?" asked another.

"Hold on, everyone! And don't get ahead of yourself, Andrew. We overhead Terry on the phone speaking about U.S. real estate during the drive up, and we're having a meeting to learn more about how all of this might shake out. Nothing is etched in stone; we are just exploring the opportunity at this point," said Rob.

Laughter broke out among the group. "No secrets with kids!" exclaimed one of the parents.

Roger broke into the conversation: "Eliza and I have been considering doing the same. Just look at the decline in prices. And with the strength of the Canadian dollar, this may be the opportunity of our lifetime."

"I understand your enthusiasm," said Terry. "But keep in mind, there are a few important things you need to consider beforehand. For example, are you considering purchasing a vacation property or an investment/rental property? Have you thought about how buying a U.S. property fits into your longer-term financial plans? Real estate is a major purchase—finding and buying the property is the easy part. Although purchasing a vacation property is an investment, be careful not to confuse a lifestyle purchase with an income/rental property purchase. These different types of purchases have different purposes and considerations. For example, with an income/rental property, property management, tenants, cash flow, and filing tax returns come with the territory. It is important that you look at the big picture—what is your long-term strategy?

"Some U.S. laws may be the same as in Canada, but some may not be the same. It is very important that you be in compliance with U.S. laws. Although the U.S. and Canada share a long border and economic ties, remember, it is still a different country."

Helen said, "I have read that there are a number of foreclosed and short sale properties on the market. Are these the same thing? How do we find these opportunities?"

"My U.S. colleagues have told me that there are numerous foreclosed, short sale, and bank-owned properties available, as well as other options," said Terry. "Similar to purchasing real estate in Canada, it is prudent to determine your primary motivation—your reason for purchasing, as this will segue into the type of property, location, and price, among other considerations. If you are thinking of purchasing an investment property, ask yourself what your goals are: Do you plan to hold onto the property in anticipation of potential future appreciation and renting the property for the duration, or is yours a buy, fix, and flip strategy? If you are contemplating purchasing a vacation property, you should consider your planned lifestyle, such things as square footage, number of bedrooms and bathrooms, single-family freehold or perhaps a condo, location, amenities, and, of course, maintenance, just to name a few things. Do you plan to keep the property long term and use it during your retirement years?

"There is a great deal to think about," Terry continued. "Your reason or purpose for purchasing will impact other important decisions that you will need to consider and make. Will you be paying cash for the property, or will you need to arrange for a mortgage loan, and if so, from a Canadian or U.S. lender? Have you thought about titling, insurance, and property maintenance if you are renting the property? What state and city interest you—why, and how accessible is transportation to there? Are you attracted to the prospect of investing in the U.S. because of the current opportunity to purchase real estate at reduced prices compared to levels of a couple of years ago, with a close-to-parity dollar and attractive interest rates? If you are keen to purchase, what is your exit plan?

"Each Canadian buyer should have a cross-border plan—a system—with experienced cross-border professionals assisting them along the way. Why don't we celebrate the boys' victory, and later we can set up a team meeting for anyone who has questions or wants additional information on the process. I'll introduce you to the Personal Property Purchase System, which is designed for Canadians buying U.S. real estate," said Terry.

"Sounds great!" said Rob.

After dinner, over coffee, Cathy volunteered to send out a group e-mail advising of a date, time, and place for anyone interested in learning about purchasing U.S. real estate to meet to discuss the program. Judging from the nodding heads, she could tell that the level of interest was definitely high.

CHAPTER 2

Creating Your Personal Purchase Plan

Even Cathy was surprised at the response from team Blackhawk parents who were interested in learning about buying U.S. real estate. She forwarded the e-mails and inquiries to Terry so that she could prepare a presentation. Expecting that it could be a long meeting, Cathy arranged the catering of sandwiches and soft drinks for the meeting.

Upon her review of the e-mailed comments and questions, Terry decided to divide the presentation into two main areas: purchasing real estate for personal use as vacation property, and purchasing property as an investment with the intention of realizing rental income.

Although many different areas of the purchase process overlap, there are important tax, insurance, estate planning, and asset protection considerations specific to each scenario. Terry thought it also important to discuss mortgage financing and currency conversion at the outset. And she'd better remind everyone about health and medical insurance while in the U.S—after all, with such an active group of kids in tow, there was bound to be at least one trip to the ER. And that it is also important to be wary of sales pitches thinly disguised as educational seminars for distressed real estate in the Sunbelt.

On Saturday afternoon, Cathy, Rob, and Andrew picked Terry and Michael up to head off to the next playoff game. Rob helped Terry carry the large box containing the booklets Terry had prepared for the meeting to the car. "Terry, you sure have put a great deal of work into this meeting. This booklet looks full of information," he commented.

"There is a lot of important information to cover. There were so many questions and ideas from the e-mail responses. I want to review as much as possible as everyone has a lot to consider given their own situation. My goal is to make you aware of some of the factors and issues you will want to consider, and point you in the direction of obtaining appropriate cross-border professional assistance so that you will be able to make prudent decisions based on a well-prepared plan. This helps avoid mistakes and allows for a smooth process with no unwanted surprises," said Terry.

Andrew chimed in from the backseat, "Hey, Mom, do they have hockey in Florida?"

Cathy laughed and said, "Ever hear of the Tampa Bay Lightning? They won the Stanley Cup a few years ago."

"Oh yeah, I sort of remember," said Andrew.

"That was a tough loss for the Calgary Flames," grimaced Rob.

"Besides," said Cathy, "we won't be living there full time, so you don't have to worry about joining a hockey team."

"That's true," Rob added, "but it doesn't mean that we can't go to a hockey game or two. That would be fun."

Cathy and Terry looked at one another and smiled. Upon arriving at the arena, Rob and another hockey dad carried the boxes of handouts into the meeting room. Meanwhile, Cathy checked with the caterer to ensure that the refreshments would be set up for the scheduled meeting time. Then the parents found spots in the stands and waited for their team to hit the ice.

The team had yet another exciting win, outscoring last year's champions 3–1, with an empty-net goal in the final minute. Now the Blackhawks would advance to the semifinals. After the game, the parents made their way to the second-floor meeting room at the arena—a ball-hockey game had been set up for the boys to keep them occupied. Terry circulated the handouts and introduced herself to the audience of thirteen—six couples and a single buyer.

After welcoming everyone, Terry asked each party about their specific interests in buying a vacation or investment property in the U.S. Three couples—Cathy and Rob, Mary and J.P., and Helen and Jay—were considering purchasing a second property for personal use. Eliza and Roger were interested in acquiring a property they figured they and other family would spend eight to 12 weeks a year in; they wanted to rent the property for the remainder of the time—although they did not need rental income in order to purchase a property. Both of these couples were thinking long term; that is, future retirement. Another couple, Michelle and David, were considering buying a vacation property with friends, each to have a 50 per cent share. And the final couple, Laura and Marty, and Lindsey, a single parent, wanted information on buying income property, to see if this was a pursuit they might eventually undertake.

"The handout you have been given," Terry began, "outlines an objective-oriented, systematic program that provides information and resources for Canadian buyers about some of the factors they should understand and consider before acquiring U.S. real estate. Many advertisements for seminars suggest that buying distressed U.S. real estate is a walk in the park. This is unfortunate because, without proper guidance from professionals, the purchase could turn into a nightmare. In 2011, Canadians were one of the larger groups of foreign buyers of U.S. real estate. But it is important to understand that there are different tax, estate, and other laws, along with mortgage options, titling, closing processes, and other rules. The program outlines real estate fundamentals, and includes access to the services of cross-border and other professionals who are available to help navigate you around the land mines, which most buyers are unaware even exist.

"Tonight's meeting will get you thinking about the process and help you determine if buying a U.S. real estate fits with your financial goals, as well as with your lifestyle plans. Everyone must seriously consider why they want to purchase U.S. real estate. I'm sure we all agree that the warm weather in the Sunbelt states, the decline in prices in some sectors compared with just a few years ago, and potential property appreciation are incentives. But everyone should clearly understand their commitment.

"If, after the meeting, any of you wish to pursue the program further, we can meet to formulate your own personal plan," said Terry. "Now, let's begin with a checklist—an outline of things to understand and consider."

PURCHASE PLAN ITEMS TO CONSIDER

1. Objective
   - To generate rental income (buy, hold, and rent)?
   - To realize a potential short-term gain (buy, fix, and flip)?
   - A vacation/lifestyle property?
2. Location
   - Which cities or states are your first and second choices, and why?
   - Do you have family or friends in the areas you've identified?
   - Are the choices driven by sports amenities, such as golf, sports fishing, baseball spring training, tennis, boating?
   - How will you get there? What is the ease of transportation, including proximity of airports, flight availability, ticket price?
3. Budget
   - What amount can you afford and/or would you like to spend?
   - Will it be cash purchase, a mortgage, or a line of credit?
   - What is your financial plan for the next three to five years?
   - What is your long-term plan?

4. Mortgage/Financing
   - Equity takeout from Canadian asset?
   - Purchase in U.S. dollars?
   - Mortgage arranged through a Canadian or U.S. lender?
   - Amount of down payment?
   - Source of down payment?
5. Timing
   - When would you like to buy, and why this timeframe?
6. Recreation and amenities
   - Is there accessibility to activities you like, such as tennis, golf, swimming, cycling, country club, boating, fishing, skiing, hiking, shopping, dining, or arts and culture?
   - Do you have teenage children or grandchildren, parents, grandparents, or siblings? What activities have you identified for them?
7. Type and size of property
   - Condo, townhouse, detached, link?
   - One-storey or two-storey?
   - Number of bedrooms and bathrooms?
   - Gated or ungated community? Security?
8. Ongoing maintenance
   - Projected costs (maintenance, property tax, insurance, utilities, mortgage interest costs, condo fees)?
   - Property manager or self-managed?
9. Personal use
   - Will you be renting the property part time?
   - How often do you plan to use the property?
   - Time to retirement?
   - Shared ownership?

10. Health care
    - Ease of access to health care?
    - Proximity to state-of-the-art health equipment and medical professionals?
    - Can you qualify for medical/health insurance? What will health/medical coverage cost?

After everyone had reviewed the checklist, Terry continued, "This is a starting point. It is important that you ask yourself why you want to purchase U.S. real estate—what are your goals? Are you contemplating buying a lifestyle (vacation) property or an investment property? What are your short- and long-term plans? It is important for you to determine *why*, as this will influence other considerations and decisions you make in setting up what and how you'll buy. Deciding on the reason for purchasing, setting your budget, and determining where you wish to purchase a property form the first part of your plan.

"Naturally, your budget, ongoing maintenance, and other costs will dictate the type and size of property you may purchase. It is important to determine what your vision is for you and your family and friends in terms of daily activities, as you want to ensure you are in a location and community with the appropriate amenities and activities.

"You need to ask yourselves: How often do you or your family plan to use the property—over Christmas, spring break, Easter, Thanksgiving—so, six to eight weeks a year? Or for longer periods? Do you plan to make shorter, long-weekend-type trips throughout the year? Consider the ease of transportation: proximity to major airports, flight availability, and costs.

"Are you thinking about renting out the property when you're not using it? Would you hire a property manager to find renters (short or long term) and to manage the property? If renting the property is part of your plan, you have to find out if the community, homeowners' association, or condominium permits short-term rentals and what the rules are.

"You need to know what your goals, both short and long term, are before creating and executing a plan," Terry explained. "Is this investment about locating a distressed property and holding until the economy and market improve and the property potentially appreciates, which could take time? Are you semi-retired or retiring in the near future? What factors will govern when you want to sell the property? Determine the top three reasons why you would like to purchase a U.S. property.

"Equally important is your exit strategy. Buying a property just because you think or have been told that it is cheap is not necessarily a good strategy. What is the true 'value' of the property? The property may require thousands of dollars in renovations. It could be in an undesirable area, so renting it, if this is your plan, may be difficult. An exit strategy is in essence part of a business plan, and it is a good idea to have one in place even if you are contemplating the purchase for personal use. Don't forget, this is still an investment of your hard-earned money.

"Now, if you turn to page 16, you will find a checklist—a grading system of the issues for you to consider." Terry paused for a moment to allow the group to find the checklist.

"Step back and objectively consider the listed items, then grade them in order of importance. Purchasing a vacation property can be an emotional decision for some buyers; try to objectively consider, review, and decide on as many of these factors as you can before setting your plan in motion. This will help to ensure that wise and sound decisions, rather than emotionally based ones, are made.

"Some questions follow the form. Use the space provided for your answers and to make notes."

REAL ESTATE CHECKLIST AND GRADING SYSTEM

1. Location (list your top three cities):

   a. _____

   b. _____

   c. _____

2. Why do you have a preference for these cities? (list preferences)

   a. _____

   b. _____

   c. _____

3. Your budget—how much are you comfortable spending (purchase price range) and why? (It is important that you be preapproved for financing if you require a mortgage.)

   Minimum: $ _____

   Maximum: $ _____

4. Estimated monthly budget

   Utilities: $ _____

   Repairs and maintenance: $_____

   Property taxes: $ _____

   Insurance: $ _____

   Condo fees: $ _____

   Homeowners association fee: $ _____

   Property management: $ _____

   If renting: Marketing expenses:

   $ _____

   If renting: Accounting and bookkeeping expenses:

   $_____

5. If you will have a mortgage, estimate your down payment:

   $_____

6. If the purchase will be a joint venture with others, list some of the pros and cons of this arrangement:

_____
_____
_____
_____

In the chart below, circle the level of importance for each item, 1 being very important, 5 being not important at all.

7. Transportation

Daily flights	1	2	3	4	5
Direct or non-stop flights	1	2	3	4	5
Affordable flights	1	2	3	4	5
Other modes of transportation (e.g., train)	1	2	3	4	5

8. Community amenities

Security	1	2	3	4	5
Gated community or condo	1	2	3	4	5
Golf club or country club	1	2	3	4	5
Tennis club or fitness facility	1	2	3	4	5
Health club or gym	1	2	3	4	5
Water (lake/ocean), boating, skiing, fishing	1	2	3	4	5
Swimming	1	2	3	4	5
Dining	1	2	3	4	5
Shopping	1	2	3	4	5
Activities for children/ grandchildren	1	2	3	4	5
Cinemas/theatre	1	2	3	4	5
Other: _____	1	2	3	4	5

9. Health care

Health care/hospital nearby	1	2	3	4	5

10. Weather

Weather and climate	1	2	3	4	5

11. Religion

Places of worship	1	2	3	4	5

12. How often do you, family, or friends plan to use the property, and when?

_____

_____

_____

_____

_____

13. Maintenance, including pool, pests, lawn, and landscaping. Do you plan to look after the property yourself or hire a property manager?

_____

_____

_____

_____

_____

_____

_____

14. Monthly utility bills, e.g., electricity, gas, propane, water, telephone, cable, Internet. Will you pay each monthly (via check or Internet banking) or do you plan on having a property manager handle this?

_____

_____

_____

_____

_____

_____

15. Do you plan to rent out the property when you're not using it (on a short-term or seasonal basis)? How will you find renters and arrange access and payment? Housekeeping and clean-up: Will you hire a property manager? Do you need partial rental income to facilitate the purchase?

_____

_____

_____

_____

_____

16. What size of property will you need? Consider how many people will be using the property (family, friends, other), and the minimum required number of bedrooms and baths. Do you want a fully detached house, a townhouse, link, a condo apartment? A gated community, adult community, golf club community, water access, tennis and health (gym) facilities? What amenities are you seeking within your community?

_____

_____

_____

_____

_____

_____

_____

17. Do you prefer brand-new or resale, and why?

_____

_____

_____

_____

_____

_____

(Continued)

18. What is your ideal plan if purchasing with other people—consider split time use, and who is responsible for what? How to share costs and maintenance?

_____

_____

_____

_____

_____

_____

The room was silent. Terry paused for a moment before continuing, "If you think you would prefer a detached property, you need to consider lawn maintenance, pest control, pool maintenance. Again, will you look after the property yourself or hire a property manager? Would you prefer a gated community with an HOA—a homeowners association? Or is a condominium apartment or condominium townhouse where much is managed for you more appropriate?

"Do you plan on purchasing a property with partners—that is, shared ownership? Consider agreements on time usage and cost-splitting. You should consider having a plan in place—in writing—for issues such as if one partner wishes to sell in the future. These issues should be put on the table and discussed and decided on before you purchase.

"You will want to work with a team of professionals, such as a cross-border attorney and accountant; an experienced U.S. real estate professional; a home inspector and possibly pool, termite, pest, and other specialty inspectors; an insurance agent; a local real estate attorney; perhaps a contractor if renovations or improvements are required; and a property management professional if you are planning to rent the property. Have you given thought as to how you will find these professionals? These are all important factors to consider.

"Working through the form and questions will take time. But it is a good starting point. This will help you to begin formulating your own plan," said Terry.

"The checklist will help us to identify our priorities," said Cathy. "But how can I determine what it will cost for a property, in locations that are our preference, that will meet my wants and needs, and the type of property—whether it is a detached four bedroom, three bath, or a two bedroom, two bath condo, waterfront, near the beach?"

"Great question. Before I answer that question specifically, let me talk for a minute about housing averages and how they can be misleading. In a nutshell, beware of national or state housing average prices. Ideally you should work with a real estate professional in the location you wish to purchase, who will provide you with prices and other information specific to your desired location and communities of choice. The fundamentals that support housing values differ from neighbourhood to neighbourhood, never mind from town to town or city to city. You may want to begin with listing your needs and wants in a property and location—this is a good starting point. This you can do with the Buyer Property Profile (see page 24).

"Now, back to your question about cost. Really, the question here is one of budget. Consider your budget based on a combination of what you qualify for and what you are comfortable spending. A good place to begin is to determine—and the lender will help you establish this—what you are comfortable spending each month for PITI (principal, interest, taxes, and insurance) based on your short- and long-term financial goals and other financial obligations. Once you have decided on this amount, you can work this number backwards and determine, based on current borrowing rates, a spending comfort zone.

"A Canadian lender will use preset underwriting criteria, such as GDS (gross debt service) and TDS (total debt service) ratios, to determine the amount of loan you qualify for. Real estate values have

declined these last few years—in some cities by 50 per cent or more—
and interest rates remain attractive. As well, the Canadian dollar is
trading close to parity, give or take a few cents. You will get more
for your money today than you would have a few years ago. Think
about what you are comfortable spending every month. Obviously,
the larger the down payment, the less the monthly carrying costs.
Depending on the lender, and whether it is a Canadian or U.S. lender,
down payment amounts may range from 10 to 35 per cent.

"You may want to speak with a Canadian lender and a U.S.
lender, as each will have different products and underwriting criteria.
The currency exchange rate of the Canadian dollar versus the U.S.
dollar at the time you purchase may be a factor in deciding whether
to have a mortgage in Canadian or U.S. dollars, as will be explained
in a few minutes. Keep in mind that some Canadian banks have U.S.
counterparts. Once you have gathered information and understand
your mortgage loan options, as well as the pros and cons of each,
you are then in a position to make a prudent, objective decision on
how to proceed. The financing and purchase-price decision will be a
factor in deciding on the type of property you are able to purchase
relative to the city you want to buy in."

"How do we find professionals, such as real estate agents, lawyers, accountants, and the like to assist with the buying process?
I don't know where to begin or whom to contact," said Helen.

"When selecting your team," Terry replied, "of course you want
professionals who are knowledgeable and experienced—but you
also want to work with professionals you feel comfortable with.
Finding and working with professionals experienced with cross-
border law and tax is important. And, similar to here at home,
ideally you want a real estate broker who listens, asks questions,
provides you with relevant information, and is genuinely interested
in assisting you with your purchase. Some buyers speak or meet
with a couple of professionals, compare the services they provide,
and then determine whom they wish to work with. I have access to

a national network of experienced U.S. real estate professionals who are available to assist you.

"Some condominiums as well as gated communities require that the buyer be approved prior to the transaction closing. The approval can take up to 30 days (or longer) after receipt of a properly completed application or document. Ensure that sufficient time is built into your contract to allow for this approval process. Also consider making the agreement conditional on your being approved. You may need to make another trip to your chosen location prior to the closing to meet condominium or HOA personnel as part of the approval process. Consult with your real estate professional and attorney for information and assistance.

"Consider following a plan—a system. And you should spend the time to gather information, establish goals, and plan ahead. This may be a vacation property—a lifestyle purchase—but it is also an investment. Developing an organized, well-thought-out plan, as well as spending time doing your own research and due diligence, will give you the knowledge and confidence to make wise decisions.

"Now, I think it's time for a break. There are some refreshments, so help yourselves and let's regroup in 10 minutes."

BUYER PROPERTY PROFILE

Name(s): _____

Address: _____

Home #: _____ Cell #: _____

Business #: _____

E-mail: _____

What is your budget? _____

Number of occupants in the home:

Adults: _____

Children: _____

What are your accommodation needs?

Number of bedrooms required? _____

Number of bathrooms required? _____

Family room/great room? _____

Kitchen: Fully modernized or more basic? _____

Kitchen: Eat-in? _____

Open-concept living room? _____

Formal dining room? _____

Main-floor laundry/Second-floor laundry? _____

What type or style of house do you prefer?

- Detached
- Semi-detached
- Link
- Townhouse
- Freehold townhouse
- Apartment
- Two-storey
- Bungalow or one-storey
- Split-level

- Multi-level
- Ranch
- Modern
- Victorian
- Country
- Heritage

Additional comments: _____

_____

_____

_____

_____

_____

Desired options/amenities:

- Fireplace
- Central air conditioning
- Central vac
- Pool/Hot tub
- Garage: number of spaces: _____
- Waterfront
- Boathouse
- Deck
- Garden
- Acreage
- Separate workshop
- Hardwood floors
- Type of appliance: _____
- Type of heating: _____
- Lot facing direction: _____
- Other: _____

Why are you considering purchase of a property?

Investment (rental income):

_____

_____

_____

_____

Vacation (second property):

_____

_____

_____

_____

What is your ideal timing, and why?

_____

_____

_____

_____

_____

How long have you been looking? List reasons why you haven't made a purchase to date.

Any challenges?:

_____

_____

_____

_____

_____

_____

_____

What neighbourhoods do you prefer, in what geographic locations?

_____

_____

_____
_____
_____
_____

Do you want to be near or on the waterfront?

☐ Yes   ☐ No   ☐ Why? _____

Do you want to live in a gated community? Do you have any specific communities in mind (if so, which)?

_____
_____
_____
_____
_____
_____

Are you willing to undertake renovations to the property?

_____

How extensive?

_____
_____
_____
_____
_____
_____

Do any family members have a special interest or requests that would be an important factor?

_____
_____
_____
_____

_____

_____

Do you plan to rent the property? Details?

_____

_____

_____

_____

_____

_____

Let's Talk about Mortgages

After the break, the group settled down again to business. Terry was pleased to see the level of energy in the room. "I'm glad to see everyone so excited. Now, it's time to talk about everyone's favourite subject—mortgages.

"As you see, we have a couple of special guests who have joined us, but before I introduce them, I want to give you some food for thought, so to speak. There are numerous mortgage products available on both sides of the border, all with different requirements, terms, and conditions. A common question is whether a Canadian buyer of U.S. property should obtain a mortgage from a Canadian or U.S. lender. The decision to obtain a mortgage from a Canadian or U.S. lender is a personal decision that depends on several factors, all of which should be discussed with your cross-border tax and legal, and possibly investment, professionals.

"Gathering information is important, so perhaps consider speaking first with the Canadian bank you do business with; it is often easier to deal with someone you know at your branch. Also, some Canadian financial institutions have U.S. retail counterparts, if you wish to obtain a U.S.-dollar mortgage. As far as speaking with a U.S. lender goes, you could do some research online and target a bank or two in the community where you are planning to purchase. Another option is to speak with a U.S. mortgage broker who facilitates mortgage loans for non-U.S. residents. He or she can shop the mortgage market for attractive interest rates and various terms and conditions. He or she may be aware of lenders that have mortgage products specifically designed for Canadian buyers. It's important to note that some U.S. mortgage brokers and banks may charge a separate loan origination fee, so be sure to inquire about this.

"I would like to introduce you now to Marcus and George. Marcus is a Canadian mortgage representative, and he works with a well-known Canadian lender. George is a U.S.-based mortgage professional and he works with the U.S. counterpart. He happens to be in town attending a finance and mortgage conference. Both gentlemen have been kind enough to join us today to review mortgage options. George has recently assisted one of my colleagues in acquiring a U.S.-dollar mortgage," said Terry.

George stood up and moved to the front of the room. "Thank you, Terry, for inviting me. What Terry did not tell you is that, although I am attending my company's conference downtown, I am also 'home.' Yes, I was born and raised here; about six years ago I took a corporate transfer to Florida, as my wife wanted to be close to her family. Over these last six years, especially the last two, I have assisted a number of Canadians with U.S.-dollar mortgage financing.

"Before I relocated to Florida, I was a mortgage professional in Toronto. I understand the differences between Canadian- and U.S.-lender mortgage products and financing, having had experience working with both types. I am looking forward to sharing information with you about the process of obtaining a U.S. mortgage."

George handed out a few loose papers and then continued, "To begin the preapproval process, my lender requests the following items, as outlined on the handout. The requested information verifies your income, assets, debts, and residence history. Organizing the paperwork is only part of the process of securing a mortgage for your property; it's important to keep the process on track, and know what steps need to be taken."

Mortgage Checklist

1. Copies of the last two months' checking and savings accounts statements and line of credit balances.

2. A copy of investment statements (stocks, bonds, GICs, RRSPs, RSPs). Lenders are looking for funds for deposit, down payment, and cash reserves, and where these funds are coming from.

3. Copies of last two years' T-4s and two recent pay stubs.

4. Copies of last one or two years' business T-1s (if applicable).

5. A copy of your primary residence tax bill and a copy of your home insurance cover page.

6. A copy of your most current mortgage statement (if you have a mortgage on your principal residence) and a list of any vehicle payments.

7. A copy of driver's license and photo ID or passport.

8. A copy of social insurance card (for a credit check).

Once you have a signed purchase contract the lender will also require:

9. A copy of canceled earnest money (the deposit toward the purchase of the real estate) check or wire.

10. A signed credit card authorization or a check payable to the lender for appraisal and other fees.

George proceeded to explain the mortgage process. "The handout summarizes the steps in the mortgage process; you can read along with me."

Mortgage Process

Step 1

The first step after reviewing your finances, including your Canadian credit history, is to ascertain what loan amount you qualify for. We will also need to look at the costs of ownership, including mortgage payment, property taxes, insurance, and homeowners or other association dues.

This, in conjunction with your current expenses in Canada, will show your debt-to-income ratio. These ratios are used to calculate what you can afford and to check that all the numbers are correct and in line. It includes all of your monthly expenses, plus your proposed expenses totaling less than 45 per cent of your monthly income. The lender can then give you a prequalification letter for the purchase price range you qualify for.

Step 2

After you find a property and put an offer on it, the lender reviews the contract and sends an application and required disclosures for your review and signature. This will include a good faith estimate (GFE). The GFE outlines a breakdown of all the costs you will incur for the purchase. It is prudent to ensure the offer and accepted contract include a mortgage finance condition that protects you. The condition is that you are able to acquire suitable financing. Your real estate professional or lawyer will assist you with this condition.

Step 3

Once your offer has been accepted by the seller, your lender will order an appraisal on your behalf and at your expense. At this point, your employment and deposit accounts are verified. An appraisal of the property and title work is ordered to verify the value of the property and check for current lien holders on the property.

Step 4

It is at this time that the loan officer will be in touch with you regarding locking the rate. Once the rate is locked with the mortgage program you have chosen, that rate is guaranteed for a predetermined timeframe to close the loan. After that time, the rate is no longer guaranteed. Make sure you find out what the lock-in timeframe is. With U.S. banks, if you do not close within the lock period, you may be charged for an extension.

Rate lock periods can be as short as 15 days and as long as 120 days (the longer locks can become very costly). Keep in mind that different rate lock periods may come with different rate quotes. This process can take 5 to 10 days or longer. Ask your mortgage professional for specific details and a time schedule.

Step 5

Underwriting: the loan is submitted to the underwriting department for review prior to approval. Once the loan is approved to close, you are notified. Closing documents are prepared and sent to the closing location.

Step 6

Closing: In the U.S., it is customary for the borrower to attend the closing. However, the closing may be negotiated by mail or power of attorney (POA). The POA may need to be approved before closing. The paperwork presented at closing is extensive and requires the signature of borrowers. You need to notify the loan officer as well as your attorney if you cannot attend the closing so that they can set up a process for the loan to close without you there. Some state laws may require the lender to have completed documentation prior to funding.

Keep in mind that if this is a freestanding house, you as the owner may be required to have your premium for the first year of property insurance paid at the time of closing.

The meeting room was quiet as the participants took notes. Then Lindsey asked, "Are the rates and costs the same with a U.S. lender as they are in Canada? I've heard that the lending rates in the U.S. are low; is this only for U.S. residents?"

"I can't speak for Canadian lenders—I will leave that to Marcus. However, currently, interest rates are what I would call attractive in the U.S.—you will have to judge this for yourself, though. Remember, to find out what the lock-in timeframe is, ask your mortgage professional," answered George.

"Before I answer your questions," Marcus said, "I want to thank Terry for the opportunity to present my lender's mortgage options. It is a pleasure to assist fellow Canadians realize their U.S. real estate goals and dreams. In answer to your question, keep in mind that although the U.S. is our neighbour, rules and regulations are different. U.S. mortgages may share some similarities with Canadian mortgages, but there are also differences. For example, in Canada, payments are normally based on an amortized timeframe and set interest rates for a term. Typically, the term and amortization in Canada are different, with the term usually being shorter than the amortized timeframe."

"In the U.S., with a conventional mortgage, often the term and amortization are the same, usually 15 or 30 years. You can also get a variable-rate mortgage in the U.S., as you can in Canada. The rate may adjust annually based on an index, and while it may start out as an attractive, low rate, it could rise to make payments more expensive later," added George.

Marcus continued, "Options you may have for arranging financing in Canada include through a line of credit on your home or by refinancing an existing mortgage already on the home or, if your home is free and clear, by putting a new mortgage on your property. In each case, you will be required to complete a mortgage application and provide income verification, as well as other documentation, such as a credit score and disclosure of liabilities."

Canadian versus U.S. Lenders

"I understand that Canada and U.S. lenders have different mortgage products, which include different rules, terms, and conditions. However, I am finding that it is a challenge to find a U.S. lender that is willing to lend to a Canadian who is purchasing a property for investment—rental—purposes," said Laura.

"There are a few U.S. institutions that will provide investor loans for Canadians," George replied. "Often these loans require a higher down payment than a vacation or second property loan and have higher interest rates. Investors loans may also have different terms and conditions than loans for a vacation or second property for personal use."

"We are considering purchasing an investment property and want to be able to deduct the mortgage interest. We understand that the U.S. property needs to be the collateral," added Marty.

"My firm has different terms, conditions, and criteria that we use with investment property loans. For example, if you are considering purchasing a condominium property, the condominium needs to be warrantable—meaning we need to review the financials and other aspects of the property. Single family is assessed different from a condominium property. In addition, the type of product and the difference in term versus amortization that is available for an investment property may be different from that for a vacation property," explained George.

Laura replied, "One of the other issues I am finding is that of titling the investment property in something other than our personal names. We are even willing to offer a personal guarantee, along with a large down payment. Next week we are meeting with our lawyer and accountant to try to find a solution."

"Yes, this can be a challenge," George agreed.

Open versus Closed Mortgage

Then Terry spoke up. "Another consideration is whether the mortgage is fully open, or closed, as this could affect you should you want to accelerate paying down the mortgage quicker. Marcus, can you comment on this?"

Marcus nodded. "This may be different in Canada versus the U.S. With an open mortgage, often there is no penalty for paying off the mortgage early. With my company, open mortgages are usually for shorter terms—six months to two years. A closed mortgage is different; normally you are committed for a predefined period, such as one to 10 years, and your interest rate is often same for this timeframe.

We call this the 'term.' Perhaps you have encountered this with an existing home here in Canada.

"Some closed mortgages include a prepayment privilege that allows you to prepay up to a certain predetermined amount annually—in addition to your required mortgage payment—without a penalty. Typically, the prepayment maximum amount represents a percentage of the original amount borrowed; for example, the mortgage terms may allow you to prepay up to 10 per cent, or 15 per cent of the original mortgage, without a penalty. So if the original amount borrowed was, say, $200,000 and your mortgage terms allow a 15 per cent annual prepayment, this means that you could prepay $30,000 ($200,000 × 15 per cent) annually without a penalty. However, often, after a certain annual prepayment percentage allowance, you may be required to pay a penalty for early payoff. Be sure to ask your Canadian lender about the rules and/or penalties regarding an early payoff of any mortgage."

"On the other side, many U.S. mortgages may allow the borrower to pay off the entire amount of the mortgage loan at any time with no penalty," said George. "This is because U.S. banks usually have origination fees or other fees not incurred by a borrower in Canada."

Terry took a sip of water and then said, "To echo what George said, you must find out if there are any additional costs with a U.S. lender, such as loan origination fees, appraisals, points, etcetera. On the positive side, U.S. lenders want good-quality borrowers with a healthy down payment."

George added, "Many U.S. lenders, especially those with Canadian counterparts, like dealing with Canadians, as their default rates are very low. Generally, Canadians don't buy vacation property for personal use in another country unless their finances are in place. Ideally, the location should be stable economically and in other ways, with a solid asset base and employment. Canadians also tend to have a home in Canada with equity. From a U.S. lender's perspective, these are the conditions for a relatively low-risk loan. Of course, the U.S. lender, or any lender for that matter, will still require documentation stating your assets, income, and liabilities, along with credit scores, as the lender needs to do its own due diligence and determine its risk."

Currency Exchange Rate

"Another factor that may impact your decision about whether to obtain a loan from a Canadian lender or from a U.S. bank is currency exchange rates. It's difficult to speculate on what the exchange rate will be tomorrow or next week—this will just drive you crazy. Think about when the Canadian dollar was trading at 60 cents to the U.S. dollar; you would have been ecstatic if you could do a currency exchange at 95 cents to the U.S. dollar at that time. We'll discuss currency exchange rates as they relate to mortgage options a little later on; however, you will want to consider and minimize currency risk. The exchange rate at the time you are purchasing may be only one of the factors in deciding which country to take out the mortgage in," Terry said.

Term and Amortization

Marcus continued, "In Canada, most of us are familiar with the *standard* or *traditional* mortgage whereby payments are amortized over a certain period—normally 15, 20, 25, or 30 years—while the term is the timeframe for which the interest rate is locked in. In Canada, your mortgage could have a term ranging anywhere from a short six-month term to a term of one to 10 years. And the rates vary depending on the term. When the term expires, the borrower renews (if he or she still requires a mortgage) at the current interest rate. The borrower bears the risk of any interest rate change."

George nodded, adding, "In the U.S., *conventional* or *traditional* mortgages are available, but some differences exist; a U.S. conventional mortgage that does not separate the term and the amortization is usually available for a vacation property. That is, your term and amortization are the same—15- or 30-year fixed-rate mortgages—and you may have the opportunity to pay off the loan early with no penalty. Other options also exist, with terms of 5, 7, or even 10 years, and the amortization for 15 or 30 years."

Fixed- versus Adjustable-Rate U.S. Mortgages

George continued, "As you may have experience with in Canada, a fixed interest rate does not change for the entire term of the mortgage. In the U.S., *adjustable rate* mortgages are also available. In the U.S. (depending on the terms of your mortgage), the mortgage interest rate can adjust once a year, based on an index such as U.S. Treasury bill rates. Then the monthly payment adjusts as well. Some adjustable rate mortgages will lock in a fixed rate for a specified number of years and then start adjusting each year. In essence, they are variable rate mortgages after the predetermined fixed period expires. It is important to understand exactly what the predetermined fixed period is for the rate to be locked in, and whether there is a cap on how much rates can move in any one year, as well as over the life of the loan.

"You might also want to be aware of the rate to which the mortgage is indexed. While many lenders use Treasury rates, some may use the LIBOR index, and others may use the cost of funds index, or COFI. The LIBOR rate—LIBOR is an acronym for London interbank offered rate—is the calculation of the average interest rate the leading banks in London, England, charge when they lend to other banks and may be used as a benchmark to which financial institutions and mortgage lenders fix their own interest rates. At the end of the initial term, your rate will be calculated by adding the margin (established at the onset of the mortgage) and the index, thus equaling the rate for that year. That is, margin plus index equal rate."

Marcus added, "In Canada, the Bank of Canada sets its overnight rate, which is the rate it lends to the banks, and then the banks add their spread, and this results in what is known as the prime rate. When the Bank of Canada changes the rate it lends, the Canadian banks often follow suit with their prime rate, which affects the variable rate of your mortgage. Not all financial institutions use the term 'prime rate' for their mortgages; some use the terms 'base rate' or 'mortgage prime rate,' which could have different definitions or rates off which they use to lend. Check with the lender to find out if it uses 'bank prime' or a different altered version and what its definition is.

"In Canada, depending on the terms of the mortgage, the banks' adjustment of their prime rate—or altered version of prime rate, where applicable—could affect your mortgage in one of a couple of ways: (a) the monthly mortgage amount you pay may change when the interest rate changes; or (b) the monthly mortgage amount does not change (remains fixed), but the percentage attributed toward interest and principal repayment changes—meaning your amortization period changes.

"Another option in Canada is to consider a *convertible* mortgage, which is in essence a variable rate or short-term (e.g., six to 12 months) *fixed-rate* mortgage that you are able to convert to a longer-term fixed rate mortgage at some time during the term. If you think that interest rates may rise in the future; having this type of mortgage allows you to take advantage of the current low rates on short-term or variable mortgages but offers you the ability to convert to a longer-term fixed rate mortgage. Consult with your mortgage professional or lawyer to ensure that you understand the terms, conditions, restrictions, and options you may have with your mortgage."

Balloon and Interest-Only Mortgage

George took over from Marcus: "If you are offered a *balloon* mortgage, it's essential that you know what kind of mortgage this is before choosing this option. With a balloon mortgage you may get a fixed low rate for three, four, or five years (the number of years may vary), but then you will need to refinance the entire balance at the end of that term. The lender may offer attractive low rates at the time you take out financing, but you could be stuck trying to refinance when rates are higher. And be careful of *interest-only* mortgages that offer low, attractive payments but may require you to refinance if money is tight or rates are higher down the road."

"Are you saying that mortgage rates may fluctuate over time?" asked Michelle.

"Typically, U.S. conventional mortgage rates are often fixed for a period. A conservative option to finance your property is with a fixed-rate 15- or 30-year mortgage. The shorter 15-year term will require a higher monthly payment, but you have the advantage of owning your property free and clear of a mortgage in a shorter time," answered George. "If you're planning to keep this property in your family for a while, you may want to consider locking in today's current rates for the entire term of the mortgage."

"Keep in mind that with interest rates at current levels, it is likely that if you have an adjustable-rate mortgage, over time the mortgage index may increase, which means that in the future, your interest rate will go up and your monthly mortgage payment will increase," cautioned Marcus.

"I guess it would be wise to get a mortgage that has a longer locked-in period up front to provide peace of mind that the interest rate is fixed and we are not exposed to a large rate increase," offered Cathy.

Marcus responded, "That will depend on your financial goals and your cash flow. A mortgage with a longer predetermined fixed period may come with a higher fixed rate. It is important for you to ask the lender these questions and understand your options. If you wish to have the security of knowing that your mortgage payments are fixed for a longer period, then, yes, this is something that you want to evaluate, and you may want to consider a longer-term fixed product.

"When you are reviewing the terms of your mortgage, make sure that you understand your options, rates, and annual adjustment terms before selecting the mortgage product. Consideration of your long-term cash flow, retirement goals, and financial budget will enable you to determine the most appropriate product. Interest rates are attractive compared with just a few years ago, both in the U.S. and Canada, and U.S. real estate prices have declined some 30 to 50 per cent, or possibly more, in some Sunbelt and other cities since the peak, making your investment more affordable. I don't have a crystal ball, so I caution you to anticipate a rate increase sometime in the future; factor this into your decision on your lock-in term."

Mortgage Origination Fee, aka Points

George stated, "It is common in the U.S. mortgage marketplace for the lender or mortgage professional to charge a loan origination fee. Origination points are charged to recover some costs of the loan origination process. One point equals 1 per cent of the mortgage loan amount. For example, if you were charged one point on a $100,000 loan, you would pay $1,000. Points are outlined on your good faith estimate (GFE), which all lenders in the U.S. must provide.

"Another way points can be presented in a loan is as a discount point. A borrower may decide to pay a point or points up front to lower or buy down the interest rate. A general rule of thumb is that one full discount point lowers your fixed interest rate by 0.25 per cent. Discount points lower the interest rate for the entire term of the loan. This option is not often used in the current market. I suggest that you discuss the two scenarios with your mortgage professional so that you are clear on all costs and types of points."

"I don't think we paid points or a fee to our mortgage professional when we obtained our Canadian mortgage. Is this only applicable to U.S. mortgages?" Michelle asked.

"Excellent question," said Marcus. "Keep in mind that every lender has costs to originate a new loan—both in Canada and the U.S. These costs are included somewhere, whether they be itemized up front or included in the interest rate. Your mortgage professional may not have charged you a fee up front for setting up your Canadian mortgage; however, recognize that he or she was paid from somewhere along the line, possibly from the yield of the interest rate."

Strategies to Pay off Your Mortgage Faster

Marcus wrapped up his talk with advice about cost-saving strategies, which got everyone's close attention. "Be sure to find out if there is a penalty to pay off part or all of the mortgage before the end of the amortization period. As George has told us, most U.S. mortgages have no prepayment penalty. Canadian mortgages usually charge a penalty for early payoff if you exceed a predetermined annual percentage allotment, as opposed to the U.S. style of charging points and bonuses up front."

"This is important to understand. Our goal is to pay off the mortgage as soon as possible," said Rob.

"Paying off debt, especially nondeductible debt, as soon as possible is wise," responded Marcus. "I suggest buyers with a mortgage—especially if it is not deductible—try to incorporate a mortgage acceleration or elimination plan, which is a regular and systematized program to accelerate through your mortgage amortization to pay off the mortgage faster and save money in interest costs.

"Depending on your amortization, the amount of your principal and interest components will vary. The longer your amortization is, usually the higher the interest portion of your payment will be in the first few years of your mortgage, as most of the monthly payment is attributed toward interest, with some going toward the principal repayment. There are a few ways to accelerate payments that flow to principal repayment, and doing so, you will save money and pay off the loan sooner.

"Common ways of accelerating through the amortization schedule include (a) adding a little extra money to your required monthly mortgage payment each month and instructing the lender to apply this extra prepayment directly to principal repayment; (b) making a yearly lump-sum payment that goes directly to principal repayment; and (c) paying bi-weekly (if a Canadian mortgage), which in essence means you make one extra mortgage payment a year.

"A combination of any of these three can have dramatic results in paying off the mortgage loan faster. Over the years, numerous borrowers who have followed a mortgage- or debt-acceleration program have commented on how easy it was to be disciplined enough to follow the process. They were delighted with the money they saved and the fact that they paid off their mortgage loan sooner."

"This is terrific. Is it really possible?" asked Mary.

"I am told that some lenders will automate it so you don't have to think about it," said Terry.

Marcus nodded, adding, "That is correct—and regular prepayments of principal in addition to your required mortgage payment does accelerate you through your mortgage, helping to pay off the mortgage debt sooner. However, it is important that you have the ability within the terms of your mortgage, whether it is a U.S. or Canadian mortgage, to make periodic prepayments of principal to your mortgage. This is something you will need to check with the lender."

Terry decided everyone needed a break, so the parents could check on the boys. "Let's take 15 minutes, everyone!"

CHAPTER 4

Only in America, You Say?

Deducting the Interest on Your Mortgage

Once the group had reassembled, Terry continued, "We have covered a great deal about mortgages, including the various options that you might consider. George will introduce you to a different type of mortgage loan product, one that may offer you the ability to deduct the interest you pay on the loan. Take it away, George," Terry said with a smile.

George moved to the front of the group. "As a general rule, U.S. citizens who reside in the U.S. and have a mortgage are often able to deduct a portion or possibly all of the interest from their mortgage loan on their personal tax returns. Canadians are normally not able to deduct the mortgage interest of their personal residence on their income tax returns. There may be a few exceptions, though."

Nonrecourse Mortgage

George paused for a moment, then continued, "One mortgage loan you may not have heard about is the nonrecourse mortgage. The term 'nonrecourse' means that if a borrower defaults on the mortgage, the lender can only go after the real property for payment; the lender cannot put a lien on, or acquire, any of the borrower's other assets. The lender has recourse only against the property, and there is no further liability if the value of the property does not satisfy the debt. Though I don't tell you this with the expectation that anyone is going to default on their mortgage."

Cathy remarked, "As it turns out, I have an uncle who owns a vacation property in Miami, and when we were visiting him, he tried to explain something about deducting the interest paid on the mortgage if you have this type of mortgage loan. It all sounded rather confusing. Can you explain how this works?"

"Well," said George, "let's say you decide on a U.S. nonrecourse mortgage for your U.S. property. In essence, as long as the equal amount of cash (from the mortgage) is invested in Canada in an income-producing instrument, the mortgage interest may be deductible. You want to consider the currency exchange at that time, as well as be comfortable with the investment. Ideally you want the income in Canada to be enough to offset the interest amount.

"This type of mortgage usually carries a higher interest rate than a traditional mortgage and requires a larger down payment. You may also be required to have the property appraised every few years, and if the equity falls below the pre-established and required loan-to-value, you may be required to top up the difference in cash. You need to ensure that the investment environment is worth it, as well as consider the risk. In addition, sometimes it is difficult to obtain a nonrecourse mortgage."

The Relationship between Estate Taxes and a Nonrecourse Mortgage

"There are similarities to buying real estate in the U.S. and Canada," George continued to explain. "However, there are different tax and estate laws in the U.S. If a Canadian resident who is not a U.S. citizen or green card holder dies, his or her estate may be subject to U.S. estate tax on the fair market value of his or her U.S. assets. Generally, in 2012, U.S. estate tax is payable only if the deceased's U.S. assets are greater than US$60,000 and the worldwide estate is greater than US$5 million. If these two thresholds are exceeded, then the primary types of U.S. assets that may be subject to U.S. estate tax are personally owned U.S. real estate and personally owned shares of U.S. corporations.

"If there is a regular or traditional mortgage outstanding upon death on a U.S. property owned by a deceased Canadian individual, the U.S. tax rules normally allow only a fraction, if any, of the outstanding amount of a regular mortgage against that property owned by the deceased to reduce the amount of U.S. real estate subject to U.S. estate tax.

"But if the mortgage outstanding is a nonrecourse mortgage, the entire value of the nonrecourse mortgage—dollar for dollar—can be applied to reduce the value of the U.S. real estate that is subject to U.S. estate tax. The nonrecourse mortgage can result in substantial U.S. estate tax savings."

Marcus added, "In the current economic environment, it may be difficult to obtain a nonrecourse mortgage from a bank. I know that you're looking forward to a happy vacation property and not thinking about the tax problems that could be created by the death of an owner. Still, this is something you should be aware of, and you need to consider implementing a strategy to protect yourself and your family. It is also prudent to speak with a cross-border attorney about estate issues and solutions, as they may present you with other strategies to consider."

The room was quiet as everyone absorbed this information. Then Rob said, "I had no idea there are potential U.S. estate tax considerations. What happens if someone buys a property without a mortgage? Would this mean they are exposed to the full value of the U.S. property for U.S. estate tax, as there is no mortgage to insulate them?"

"Great question. This is a topic for another meeting, and one I think would be best answered by a cross-border legal professional. Perhaps I can arrange this for another meeting," said Terry.

Currency Decisions

Marcus continued, "One other important consideration is the currency exchange rate at the time you are purchasing. When the Canadian dollar is above 90 cents to the U.S. dollar, consideration should be given to taking either an equity mortgage or line of credit from your Canadian property, converting these funds to U.S. dollars, and buying the U.S. vacation property with all cash. Alternatively, if you have a Canadian business or another asset that you can borrow against (check with your accountant and/or financial professional to determine if this is appropriate), these may be other potential options. In so doing, you will be paying the loan with Canadian dollars—minimizing risk that the Canadian dollar will decline. You know ahead of time what your worst-case scenario is relative to the currency.

"Ultimately, you want to mitigate the currency risk, and with a 90-cent or greater Canadian dollar, this is certainly a factor. Keep in mind that the higher the Canadian dollar is against the U.S. dollar, the greater the risk becomes on the downside. I don't know how high the Canadian dollar may rise, nor do I know when, by how much, or for how long—it may decline."

"So, if we are comfortable with the current rate of currency exchange, in essence we remove any downward currency risk if we have a Canadian loan?" David thought out loud.

"If you receive rental income on the property, you are required to file annual tax returns in both Canada and the U.S., and the accountants would figure out the currency along with the appropriate deductions. If you are considering purchasing an investment property to rent, it is important that you consult with mortgage, tax, and estate professionals, as this is a different scenario than purchasing a vacation property, which may require different considerations and solutions. Tax and accounting is another topic, but suffice it to say the currency would be factored into the tax filings on your Canadian return both for income and on the future sale of the property," replied Marcus.

"There are different options for everyone depending on the purpose of your purchase, as well as on your short- and long-term plans. Today, you have been given an overview of some of the mortgage products available. My suggestion is to review and discuss these options with your lender or mortgage broker and have them help you select a product that will work for your individual needs and goals. Consider your short- as well as long-term plans and the currency exchange rate, and ensure that you get everything in writing," said Marcus.

CHAPTER 5

How to Hedge Exposure to Currency Risk

"Could you explain more about currency exchange?" J.P. asked. "It seems to be a consideration when you buy and also when you pay your mortgage, as well as in terms of property expenses."

"It's difficult to pick the best time to exchange Canadian money for U.S. dollars. Many Canadians focus on how much they think they will 'lose' and whether they should wait until the next week to find out if the loonie goes up another cent or two. Of course, it seems that as soon as you do the exchange, the next day the Canadian loonie goes up. Conversely, if the loonie goes down, you are upset that you didn't exchange more Canadian money to U.S. dollars," replied George.

"Yes, that has happened to me. Just when I think I've got the best exchange rate, the next day, the loonie is up again," commented Jay.

"It's almost pointless speculating on what the exchange rate will be tomorrow or next week—it is what it is. Trying to time currency fluctuation will drive you crazy. I have no idea where the Canada-U.S. exchange rate will be next month, six months from now, or next year. Experienced currency traders, investment managers, and economists may even have a difficult time accurately predicting the exchange rates over any extended period. If they did know for certain, with that knowledge they would no longer need to predict or forecast," said George.

"If you consider history, the Canadian dollar has traded from 95 cents some decades ago to parity and slightly above in 2007 and now to its current level. Numerous factors influence exchange rates, making it difficult to predict where rates will go over the long term—factors such as differences in interest rates, economic growth prospects of each country, differences in productivity performance, differences in trade, current account and fiscal balances, political issues, taxation, inflation, and a host of other economic and political issues can also affect currency value.

"Simply put, it may be a function of supply and demand: if the world favours one currency over another, the more desired currency will enjoy a higher exchange rate," explained George.

Cathy asked, "So, how do we avoid trying to speculate on which way the currency will move?"

"Excellent question," commented George. "There are two things you may want to consider. First, keep in mind that the Canada-U.S. exchange rate can fluctuate 30 to 100 basis points most days. There are currency exchange tools available to take advantage of these daily fluctuations. When you are planning to convert Canadian dollars to U.S., ideally you will want to buy at the lower end of the daily fluctuation. You can make a currency bid or have an agreement with a currency broker, or perhaps a bank, to purchase a certain amount of foreign currency at some point in the future at a fixed price. A currency bid can be placed for 30 days and canceled or amended often without penalty. The risk is if the currency exchange is trending upward, your bid may never get filled.

"A second strategy you may want to consider is diversifying some of your income-producing assets and savings into U.S.-dollar-generating investments. This is a good way to hedge your future U.S. dollar requirements, as investments that generate U.S. dollars will enable you to pay for some of your expenses without having to exchange Canadian money to U.S. dollars. Do this now, well before you retire. An experienced financial professional can assist you with this strategy. This may also save you a lot of money in commissions that financial institutions charge for exchanging currency."

George paused to gauge the mood of the group before continuing. "Hedging against fluctuations in the currency is something you need to implement. For example, when you retire, if you decide to spend six months a year for the next 20 years in your U.S. property, consider that you will need approximately US$360,000, or maybe more, depending on your projected spending, in today's dollars to fund this lifestyle, assuming that you spend US$3,000 per month (six months of the year) not including inflation. If you do not think about hedging yourself now, this could become very costly. Given that the Canadian loonie is very strong against the U.S. dollar, acting now could provide you with a great deal of peace of mind.

"Over short periods, speculating on the currency may be profitable, and you may get lucky. However, over the long term, it is very difficult and risky. If you are looking for security and want to avoid second-guessing the currency, plan for this and hedge your bets."

Cathy commented, "With the decline in U.S. real estate prices from their peak and the Canadian dollar trading above the 90-cent range, you're right—it could be a mistake to assume currency rates will stay the same or even get better in the future. The real risk is not if the Canadian dollar goes up in value but, rather, if it goes down."

"That is a prudent and conservative way to look at the currency issue," said George. "The decision as to when to convert should be made according to your personal goals. If you plan to spend time in the U.S., it makes sense to consider converting at least some funds now because you know with certainty what the exchange rate is today. The Canada-U.S. exchange rate has been on quite a significant uptrend these last few years. Perhaps you might want to consider converting an amount now, avoid currency speculation, and get on with your life. The time to exchange Canadian dollars to U.S. dollars is when you can achieve your desired lifestyle in line with your financial goals. Remove the emotion and act shrewdly and deliberately."

"Where is the best place to exchange money? I've heard that banks charge a large commission. Are they really more expensive than other places?" asked Laura.

"World currency markets determine the exchange rate," said Marcus. "However, the commission or markup fees vary. If you exchange large sums of money, often the fees are less. If you choose to exchange at a bank, ask for the spot rate. To find out and compare the fees, simply compare the exchange rate, or the spot rate—which you can find online or in the newspaper—with the rate posted or offered at your bank. Keep in mind that exchange rates can vary substantially between financial institutions; it's wise to shop around.

"It's also a good idea to check with U.S. banks—you may be pleasantly surprised at the rate. Several U.S. banks are affiliated with Canadian banks, and they may exchange Canadian dollars at reduced commissions. You might want to consider opening a U.S.-dollar account with a U.S. bank that has a Canadian counterpart; I've heard that sometimes they will exchange Canadian dollars at reduced commissions in order to attract new clients.

"If you have a U.S.-dollar account in the U.S. and a Canadian-dollar account with the counterpart company in Canada, ask if the two accounts can be linked or if there is a specific way for you to transfer funds from one account to another at preferred exchange rates. These same banks may also offer banking services and can also assist you with U.S. income-producing products," Marcus continued.

"The brokerage firm I deal with offered to exchange currency at a very low commission," said Marty.

"I have also heard that brokerage firms and foreign exchange brokers offer better rates than some banks. It pays to shop around, do your research, and understand all your options," said Terry.

George offered, "One other thing to keep in mind is that using Canadian-dollar credit cards for U.S. purchases can be expensive; credit card companies generally charge 2 to 3 per cent currency exchange fees on top of transaction fees. Check your credit card statement for the exchange rate and compare this rate to the historical rate for that day; you may be surprised at the difference. You might want to consider getting a U.S.-dollar credit card. This means that you pay your credit card bill with U.S. funds. Canadian or U.S. banks can assist you with setting up a U.S. credit card."

Terry could see that the hockey parents were beginning to understand that buying a property in the U.S. requires experienced cross-border professional guidance and assistance to minimize and/or avoid income, estate tax, and potentially other problems in the future.

"We're not trying to overwhelm you with information and options. We simply want to outline the steps and some important items you should be aware of that may affect your decisions. Purchasing a property, whether it is in Canada or anywhere else, is a big investment. The goal is to eliminate unwanted surprises and help make the process run smoothly. I understand that you are not experts in this business. There are cross-border professionals to help guide and assist you throughout the process. Your first step is determining your budget, mortgage preapproval, if applicable, as well as your ideal location. The program covers many of the cross-border issues you will want to consider. Educating yourself is an important part of the process."

"That makes sense. Establishing your budget and location preference is a logical first step. It's difficult to go shopping if you don't know how much you are able to spend, and your budget will influence what you can buy," said Cathy.

"I have heard that real estate prices have declined in the U.S. and borrowing costs are reasonable," she continued. "This means we can purchase a nicer property, in a better location, cheaper than a few years ago. It seems like this is an opportunity of a lifetime. Can you tell us how to find these deals? Do we need a real estate agent in the U.S.? How does this work?"

Terry grinned and responded, "Cathy, prices have declined in some areas quite significantly from their peak and interest rates are affordable. There have been a number of foreclosures and bank sales nationwide, which has in part fueled the price decline. Compared with just a few years ago, in many cities there is a larger inventory base to choose from; all this puts a buyer in a good position to be able to better afford to purchase a property.

"It is important that you work with an experienced local U.S. real estate professional, as he or she is knowledgeable about what's happening in that particular city or town. These professionals have access to the local real estate board of which they are members, for listed property, among other resources, and, in many cases, they also have contacts with banks or lenders regarding short sales, fore-closures, and bank sales.

"It is also a good idea to work with a U.S. real estate professional who is experienced working with Canadian buyers, since, as you've learned, there are certain factors for Canadians buying U.S. property to consider. I have access to a network of U.S. real estate brokers that are experienced in assisting Canadian buyers.

"We have covered a great deal today with regards to setting your budget and financing, determining your ideal location, and complet-ing checklists. I suggest that you review the material we've covered and, for anyone interested in pursuing this further, we can set up a time to get started. You'll need to get your budget organized and pos-sibly get mortgage financing preapproval (if applicable), decide on your location, and ascertain your needs and wants. Completing the Property Profile will help you do this.

"I would like to thank Marcus and George for joining us to share this information about mortgages. I see that Marcus and George's contact information is included on the material they handed out, so feel free to connect with either of them if you wish additional infor-mation about mortgages."

"It's my pleasure, Terry. Thanks for the opportunity for George and me to share the information with you all," Marcus replied.

"Once the front-end aspects of the process we have covered are completed, the next step is researching and learning about your chosen location, including the types of property available within your budget and the facilities and amenities at that location. At that time, I can introduce you to U.S. real estate professionals who can assist you in sourcing property and educating you on the local real estate marketplace. It is important that you also be knowledgeable about U.S. tax, estate, and other issues you will need to understand as a Canadian buyer. Let's take these issues one at a time," said Terry. "Why don't we set up another meeting to review the next steps of the program? We have a lot more to cover."

"Fabulous! I can see there is a great deal to understand and think about. This is very exciting and I would really appreciate participating in another meeting," said Mary.

The room was buzzing as everyone gathered their books and packed up. Cathy announced, "I'll coordinate a time and date with Terry for the group to reconvene for our next program meeting and advise everyone."

The parents headed downstairs. The boys reluctantly broke up their game and all headed to the parking lot.

Andrew asked, "So are we buying a house in Florida, too?"

Cathy grinned. "My, aren't we excited! Well, we are thinking about it . . ."

"That would be sweet!" said Andrew.

Cathy turned to Terry. "Rob and I will review our notes and the program and do our homework. We would like to know more."

"I agree," replied Rob. "We've tossed around the idea of buying a U.S. vacation property for a year or so now—we just didn't know where to begin or whom to contact. I never considered a lot of what was brought up at the meeting today. Once we review the information, we would like to take the next steps in thinking through owning a U.S. vacation property."

Terry smiled, nodding. "Just let me know when you are ready, and I will introduce you to the appropriate cross-border professionals. Cathy, I'll call you tomorrow once I look at my schedule and let you know my availability for the next meeting."

CHAPTER 6

How to Set Up Your Budget

Cathy and Rob spent time that evening reviewing the information from the meeting and discussing acquiring a U.S. property. Both professionals with established careers, they plan to work for another 10 to 15 years. They own their principal residence in Canada mortgage-free and have RRSPs that they have contributed to yearly for the past 15 years, plus about $250,000 in liquid savings. Rob also has acquired numerous shares in the company he works for and estimates the value of these shares to be approximately $750,000. All of their vehicles are paid for, and they have no other debts.

Their plan was focused on acquiring a property in Florida. Because of the decline in prices, attractive interest rates, the strength of the Canadian dollar, and the number of properties on the market, they felt they were presented with a unique, possibly once-in-a-lifetime opportunity. And they wanted to act now because the economic and real estate situation could turn around at some point in the future. Cathy's concern was that interest rates may not remain as low in the long term, and that eventually real estate inventory and choices may decline and prices could increase.

They estimated they would use the property approximately seven to eight weeks per year. Both have family that would also use the property part of the year. They discussed renting the property part time but do not want to rely on rental income to underwrite the purchase—any rental income would be considered a bonus. They also understand that some communities in their location might not permit short-term rentals.

Rob and Cathy felt that $250,000 to $350,000 was a comfortable purchase-price range, but they wanted to speak with a mortgage professional to find out about various mortgage options. After much consideration, they decided they wanted to purchase in Orlando, Florida, as Orlando has many direct and nonstop flights, and the city offers amenities and entertainment for all ages.

"Wow, this is starting to take shape; we have the beginnings of our plan. I'm ready to talk to Terry about our thoughts and decision and pursue speaking with a mortgage lender," said Cathy.

"That's great. I hope we can find a house and be in by fall! Can you envision Christmas in Florida?" Rob replied with a grin.

"You're getting a little ahead of things, Rob. We have a lot of work to do in the meantime," said Cathy, always the practical one.

The following day, Terry contacted Cathy with a couple of possible dates for the next information meeting. Cathy also let Terry know that she and Rob were ready to move ahead in earnest. "Terry, we're ready to proceed to the next step. We stayed up last night reviewing and discussing the program and completed the property profile. We have decided that we want to speak with the mortgage lenders and get the ball rolling." Cathy explained that they wanted to purchase in Orlando, Florida, and that Rob really wanted to be in the home for Christmas.

Terry could hear the excitement and anticipation in Cathy's voice and replied, "It's clear that you and Rob have thought this through and know what you want to do; the next step is to get your budget and finances in order."

"We thought we would meet with our local bank manager to find out about our options. Rob and I are anxious to get going on the process," said Cathy.

"I am thrilled for you and Rob," said Terry.

Cathy and Rob's Mortgage Options

The next day, Cathy met with her and Rob's Canadian bank mortgage loan officer, Sylvie, to discuss arranging financing for their U.S. purchase. Sylvie presented a couple of options:

1. Create a new first mortgage for up to 90 per cent (85 per cent for equity takeout) of the appraised value of their Canadian home, which would involve a one-time default-insurance premium that would be added to the mortgage (if the loan-to-value was greater than 80 per cent).

2. Put a line of credit on the home for up to 80 per cent (depending on the location of the home) of the appraised value of the home.

Loan-to-value ratios may differ depending on the lender. Check with your lender for specifics.

Both options have pros and cons. Cathy thought that if she and Rob planned to hold the mortgage long term (5 to 10 years), the mortgage may be the best route to take, as the interest rate could be fixed for up to 10 years (if they chose a 10-year term), and generally may be a lesser borrowing cost than a line of credit if interest rates should increase. If they thought they could pay off the mortgage short term, then perhaps the line of credit would be appropriate because it is completely open, with no penalty for early payoff. Cathy was told that the mortgage strategy allowed a 15 per cent annual mortgage prepayment with no penalty if they wished to pay down the mortgage. (Note: prepayment privileges vary from lender to lender.) A line of credit could have a fixed rate component with principal and interest reduction as well. Decisions, decisions!

Annual mortgage prepayment percentages may vary depending on the lender.

Sylvie explained that if the loan-to-value is greater than 80 per cent, the mortgage is considered a high-ratio mortgage, which would require default loan insurance to insure the lender against default. This is a cost borne by the borrower. Alternatively, if the loan-to-value is less than or equal to 80 per cent of the appraised value of the existing property, this is considered a conventional mortgage and usually no default insurance premium would be charged.

"What are the rules regarding early payoff of the mortgage?" Cathy asked.

"You can choose an open mortgage, which has no prepayment penalty for early payoff, or a closed mortgage, which has an annual prepayment percentage allowance. A closed mortgage with this bank (my employer) allows you to prepay up to 15 per cent of the original borrowed amount annually each year during the term without a penalty," answered Sylvie.

Cathy and Sylvie reviewed the mortgage products available, along with interest rates based on terms ranging from 2 to 10 years.

"Rob and I will discuss the mortgage products, terms, and options, in addition to reviewing whether we want to have a mortgage or a line of credit," Cathy told Sylvie. "Once we've reviewed our budget, as well as our short- and long-term financial goals, I'll be in touch."

Later that evening, Rob and Cathy reviewed the mortgage information. They decided that they would be comfortable with a maximum purchase price of $350,000 (although they qualified for more), with 30 per cent down ($105,000), which they would source from their liquid savings.

Cathy jotted down a list of expenses they needed to consider, such as:

- flights, accommodations, and out-of-pocket expenses to visit to find a property (possibly two or three trips)
- closing costs for the transaction
- health insurance in the U.S.

- moving and decorating expenses
- furniture for the house

"We can pay for these expenses out of our liquid savings as well," suggested Cathy.

"I guess we need to decide on whether we want a mortgage or a line of credit?" Rob said.

"I'll compile the documentation that Sylvie requested and then we can discuss this with her later this week," Cathy told him. "In the meantime, I'll send an e-mail to the group advising of the next meeting, and reminding them to bring along the handouts from last time."

CHAPTER 7

Key Considerations Regarding Location

With the Blackhawks in the championship playoffs, the parents were looking forward to attending another information meeting. Cathy and Rob arrived at the arena early so that Cathy could set up for the meeting.

Terry was busy that morning meeting with another couple. David and Michelle were considering purchasing a property with friends; they planned to share usage and expenses. The two couples were avid golfers and had expressed an interest in Scottsdale, Arizona.

Michelle informed Terry that they had met with a Canadian mortgage specialist to determine their mortgage preapproval. A full mortgage application and credit check was completed and the lender was arranging for an appraisal of their Canadian home.

As the Canadian dollar was trading close to par with the U.S. dollar, Michelle and David wanted to minimize currency risk with their mortgage. They decided to do an equity takeout from their Canadian residence for their portion of the home purchase, convert it to U.S. funds, and pay cash for the U.S. property. The mortgage would be on the Canadian property. Michelle anticipated the purchase price would be in the $500,000 to $600,000 range; they would be responsible for half of the investment, and their friends would be responsible for the other half.

"Our friends are in the midst of completing the same process with their Canadian home. By the end of the week we should both have our mortgage preapprovals; then we are set to begin our house search," said Michelle.

"That's great!" responded Terry. "Have you and your friends completed the Property Profile? This will be the basis for selecting the most appropriate properties and neighbourhoods to meet your needs and goals."

"We've both completed the Property Profile. We have also set up a meeting with the cross-border lawyer to determine how to structure titling and a shared ownership agreement, as we both want everything spelled out in writing in advance," replied Michelle.

Terry responded, "Sounds like you have things under control. You might also want to discuss U.S. estate planning with your lawyer so as to avoid or at least minimize exposure to U.S. estate tax. We'll be reviewing this topic in detail during today's meeting."

"I'll add that to the list of items to discuss with the cross-border lawyer. I didn't know this was something I needed to be aware of."

"It's an important consideration, especially given the shared ownership. The cross-border lawyer can review and recommend to both couples how to structure the ownership. We will also be covering aspects of ownership today."

* * *

The arena was buzzing with excitement. Both the Blackhawks and their opponents, the Sonics, were on the ice warming up.

Cathy sat down beside Terry, wrapped in her blanket, a hot coffee in hand. "Rob and I met with our Canadian bank mortgage specialist, Sylvie," she told Terry. "We are now approved for an equity takeout mortgage on our home. We can afford and plan to put 30 per cent down, so we'll be considered as having a conventional mortgage and can avoid having to add the mortgage default insurance to our costs. And we are preapproved for a purchase price of $450,000, including the down payment, although we don't want to spend that much. We haven't decided whether we will go with a fixed or variable rate on the mortgage."

Typically, a conventional mortgage in Canada is a mortgage loan that is less than or equal to 80 per cent of the lending value. The down payment is at least 20 per cent of the purchase price or appraised value of the property. Normally, a conventional mortgage does not require mortgage loan insurance (also known as mortgage default insurance). Consult with your lender for specifics, as there may be situations where mortgage default insurance may apply.

The buzzer sounded and the hockey game began. The cheering started immediately as the Blackhawks scored within the first two minutes. Despite a number of good scoring chances on both sides, the Hawks were up by a single goal at the start of the third period.

Michelle moved over to join Terry and Cathy. "It's been a long, cold winter. I can't wait until next year when David and I have 10 weeks of holidays, and we can spend a great deal of time playing golf in the warm south. This cold weather is not for me."

"Wow, that's great!" Cathy said. "I guess Jacques will be moving on to college or university?"

"Yes. He's finished high school this semester and has been accepted into the University of Calgary, and he'll be living on campus. Our older daughter is attending the University of Arizona on a tennis scholarship; we will get to spend time with her during the winter."

Terry responded, "I thought you and David just liked the golf courses in Arizona. I had no idea that your daughter was going to school there."

"We do enjoy the golf courses and the dry desert air. David and I plan on retiring within five years and want to spend most of the winter in Scottsdale. Because of the decline in prices and the strength of the Canadian dollar, we feel this is a wonderful time to buy. We feel that if we wait too long, the economy could strengthen and prices may rise and inventory selection could decrease. Besides, we are looking forward to spending all of our holiday time in our U.S. house and, best of all, we can spend time with Jacques, cheer on Isabella during her tennis tournaments, and visit with family and friends," replied Michelle.

"Ohhh," roared the crowd as the Sonic forward hit the goal post.

"What a game! Both teams are playing very well," said Michelle. In the final minute, with the Sonic goalie pulled for an extra player, Andrew captured the puck near his blue line and made a beeline for the Sonic net. The Blackhawks bench went berserk. The Hawks were the new champions.

The boys—and their parents—high-fived one another in celebration of their championship win. Once the excitement ebbed, the parents headed for the meeting room. Cathy was busy ensuring everyone had copies of the material, while everyone helped themselves to chicken dinners and soft drinks. Terry thought that everyone would be hungry after the game and decided, much to people's surprise and delight, to have dinner delivered for the meeting. The boys were going to the coach's house for pizza.

"Does anyone have any questions from the material we covered last week?" Terry asked. "I realize we covered a lot of material. Just to refresh, the program was designed as an objective-oriented, systematic program. It is important that you are aware of cross-border rules and laws, as well as understand your options so that you can make informed decisions. The economic situation has presented you with a unique opportunity, one that we have never experienced in our lifetime. Many Canadians who had been thinking of purchasing U.S. real estate in the past are now moving forward due to many factors such as the strong Canadian dollar, the number of properties available, the decline in prices, as well as the attractive interest rates.

"There has been talk that the U.S. real estate market is starting to bottom and recover in some areas. I don't have a crystal ball, nor do I know what is going to occur in the future. U.S. real estate prices have declined these last few years, interest rates are more affordable than several years ago, and there are many properties on the market, all of which has created a great opportunity for Canadian buyers. It is prudent for you to investigate sales and pricing trends in your chosen location—remember, this is an investment as well as a lifestyle enhancement and should be approached with a well-thought-out plan."

Terry then asked the group to address the mortgage section of the handouts. "I would like to pick up from where we left off at the last meeting and review different parts of the program.

"Now that you have had a chance to review and discuss your reason for considering purchasing a U.S. property, along with deciding on the city or town, your budget, and perhaps also the type of property you are looking for, and you have a general overview of mortgage options, you are ready to consider the next steps.

"Although you may use the services of a real estate professional to assist you with finding and acquiring a property, it is still important for you to do your own due diligence. In a nutshell, be wary of national or state housing average prices. The fundamentals that support housing values differ from neighbourhood to neighbourhood, never mind from town to town or city to city. Real estate values, demand, and inventory levels are local. Regardless of which country, province, territory, or state you are buying real estate in, keep in mind the importance of 'location, location, location.'

"You want to purchase a property in an area that has a future, not a past. Ideally, you want to see positive trends. If you are unfamiliar with the city or community, you might want to do research through the local chamber of commerce on job-growth prospects and town or city improvements. Check to see if any new industry is moving into the area. Are there any residential construction projects underway? What about new commercial developments—shopping malls, strip malls, office buildings, medical facilities, restaurants, schools? Are the builders offering incentives to attract buyers? You also should research vacancy rates and available rental housing inventory. If there are high vacancy rates, find out why. This is important if you are buying an investment/rental property. Also important for an investor is transportation infrastructure—people need to get to their place of work.

"Research and review sales trends—does the data support an increase or a decrease, or is it a flat sales trend? How quickly are properties selling in the area, and what is the ratio of the number of properties that sell versus the number coming on the market? Your real estate broker will be able to provide you with information on sales trends. Research and ask questions—ideally, although there are no guarantees, you want to see your property increase in value over time and have ease of resale down the road. That's why due diligence is important.

"Once you have decided generally on a few locations, it is helpful to look at a map of the area and plot out important facilities and amenities. Where is the airport; what are the major highways and other modes of transportation, such as metro transit? Where are the health-care facilities? Where are the downtown and key shopping, dining, and entertainment areas, and other amenities that are important to your family? Having this information before considering communities will prove to be helpful in navigating."

Helen commented, "We really need to treat the research and evaluation process similar to how we would here at home."

"Although you may be excited about the prospect of finding and purchasing a vacation property for personal use, it's important to be objective-oriented and to try to make nonemotional, fact- and researched-based decisions. It is important to spend the time thinking through and determining your needs and your short- and long-term objectives, as well as your financial goals. The Property Profile included with the handout is a good starting or reference point for determining your needs and wants. The Property Profile, combined with your budget, geographic preferences, research, and due diligence will help you when it comes to evaluating the available options. It is also important to take the time to view the properties; be wary about purchasing a property that you view only on the Internet," said Terry.

CHAPTER 8

How Long Can You Stay in the U.S.?

The Nonresident Substantial Presence Test

Cathy refreshed everyone's coffee and set out a tray of sweets while the group took a 10-minute break. In the meantime, Terry greeted two people who had just arrived and escorted them to the front of the room.

As the group reassembled, Terry continued, "I would like to introduce everyone to two very special professionals who have graciously agreed to join us to discuss important factors that Canadian buyers should be aware of when purchasing U.S. property. Jonathan joins us from an international boutique law firm that specializes in cross-border law. Diana is a partner in a cross-border tax practice. Both Jonathan and Diana have prepared packages for your review and are available for a short while after tonight's meeting."

Terry returned to her seat while Diana handed out the packages. Jonathan began, "I am thrilled to be here with Diana this evening to review items that Canadians should consider when purchasing a U.S. property. Let's begin with residency rules and compliance.

"Canada generally taxes individuals based on residency, not citizenship; the U.S. taxes individuals based on citizenship and residency. U.S. citizens and green card holders are taxed on their worldwide income regardless of where they live or work. A green card holder is someone not born in the U.S. who has been granted permanent residency in the U.S. Individuals who are not U.S. citizens are called 'aliens.' As a Canadian in the U.S., you will either be recognized as a resident alien or as a nonresident alien. You need to understand this distinction, since this affects income tax filing rules and requirements.

"Nonresident aliens are normally taxed in the U.S. on their income from U.S. sources only, with some exceptions. Deductions and exemptions are limited for nonresident aliens. A resident alien is taxed in the U.S. on worldwide income, like a U.S. citizen, and is required to file U.S. income tax returns and pay tax on his or her worldwide income from all sources. A resident alien would be eligible for many of the same deductions and personal exemptions as a U.S. citizen. Keep in mind that U.S. income tax law has established laws regarding residency and how long a Canadian can stay in the U.S. each year."

Jonathan paused for a moment and then continued, "The decision as to whether you are considered a resident alien or nonresident alien depends on how long you are physically in the U.S. (whether you own real estate or not). Canadian snowbirds are treated as a resident for tax purposes if they meet either of two tests: (1) the permanent resident—that is, they hold a green card—or (2) the Substantial Presence Test.

"Let's discuss the residency test criteria, outlined in the package; just follow along with me."

RESIDENCY TEST

1. **Permanent resident**—A Canadian citizen who is a lawful permanent U.S. resident or green card holder is considered a resident for U.S. income tax purposes. Green card holders are treated as U.S. residents even if they are not physically present in the U.S. Green card holders must also file U.S. tax

returns each year regardless of whether they live or work in the U.S.

2. **Substantial Presence Test**—A foreigner may be considered a U.S. resident for tax purposes if he or she spends a "substantial" portion of the year in the U.S.

   The Substantial Presence Test is a formula under the U.S. tax law that calculates the number of days you spend in the U.S. over a three-year period. It is important to keep a written record of the number of days you are physically present in the U.S. If you exceed the limit (based on the formula), you become classified as a U.S. resident for tax purposes only. You are not considered a U.S. resident for immigration purposes. You are considered a U.S. resident for tax purposes if:

   a. You are present in the U.S. on at least 31 days during the current calendar year, and

   b. You are present in the U.S. on 183 days during the immediate three-year period, which includes the current year and the two preceding years, broken down as follows:

      • 100 per cent of the current year days (each day present in the U.S. during the current year counts as a full day), *plus*

      • 1/3rd of the days in the U.S. during the first preceding year, *plus*

      • 1/6th of the days in the U.S. during the second preceding year.

Note: The nonresident will be treated as being present in the U.S. on any day that he or she is physically present in the U.S. at any time during such day (even if you arrived late in the evening or departed early in the morning—this counts as one day). One exception is time spent in the U.S. because he or she is unable to leave the U.S. due to a medical condition that occurred while being in the U.S.

To determine if you meet the Substantial Presence Test for 2011, calculate the following:

Example 1

Number of days present in the U.S. in 2011	100
1/3rd of the number of days in the U.S. in 2010: 1/3rd of 120 days	40
1/6th of the number of days in the U.S. in 2009: 1/6th of 150 days	25
Total Days:	165

Total number of days is less than 183 days—so *not* a resident.

Example 2

Number of days present in the U.S. in 2011	124
1/3rd of the number of days in the U.S. in 2010: 1/3rd of 126 days	42
1/6th of the number of days in the U.S. in 2009: 1/6th of 150 days	25
Total Days:	191

If the total equals 183 days or more and you spend more than 31 days in the U.S. in the current year, you have met the Substantial Presence Test and are considered a resident alien for 2011. If the total is less than 183 days, you are considered a nonresident alien for 2011.

Note: The days do not have to be consecutive. You need to include days in the U.S. even if you were there for part of the day, including travel into and out of the U.S.

Jonathan noted, "As a general rule, Canadians who spend fewer than 121 days or approximately four cumulative months a year in the U.S. do not need to worry about becoming a resident of the U.S. for tax purposes under the Substantial Presence Test. Visitors are considered residents of the U.S. if they meet the Substantial Presence Test and stay for at least 183 days total in the U.S. during the three-year period—calculated as shown in the handout—that includes the current year and are required to file a U.S. tax return reporting income from all sources, including income from Canada, unless an exception applies."

Cathy asked, "If I understand this correctly, we could be taxed as a U.S. resident if we spend a substantial amount of time in the U.S. even though we do not have legal working immigration status or a visa. Is that right?"

Jonathan responded, "You could be deemed a resident for U.S. income tax purposes, but you do not have the right to actually live or work in the U.S., as this right is only granted under separate U.S. immigration laws."

Jonathan paused for a moment to allow the group to absorb the information. Then he continued, "However, exceptions exist. Canadians who meet the Substantial Presence Test may be considered nonresident aliens and exempt from U.S. income tax on their worldwide income for the current year. Exceptions exist for Canadians who do meet the Substantial Presence Test that allow them to be taxed as a nonresident. Let's take a look."

EXCEPTIONS TO THE SUBSTANTIAL PRESENCE TEST

1. **Closer connection**—For those Canadians who maintain a closer connection to a foreign country, you will not be treated as meeting the test for the current year if:

   a. You are present in the U.S. fewer than 183 days during the current year,

  b. You maintain a main "tax" home (i.e., place of business or employment—a place where you regularly live) in another country other than the U.S. during that current year, and

  c. You have a closer connection to a single other country other than the U.S. in which you maintain a tax home.

 2. **Exempt individual**—You will generally not be treated as being present in the U.S. on any day in which you are temporarily present in the U.S. as a foreign-government-related individual, a teacher or trainee who holds a J visa, a student holding a F, J, or M visa, or a professional athlete temporarily in the U.S. to compete in a charitable sports event.

Jonathan continued to explain, "Generally, an individual may establish that his or her tax home is in another country other than the U.S. by showing that the principal place of business or employment and/or the principal residence are located in that other country. This other tax home must exist for the entire taxable year and be in the foreign country that you are claiming as your closer connection.

"To determine and confirm whether you have a closer connection to another country, generally you can weigh your contacts with the U.S. against those with the foreign country, contacts such as:

- location of your regular, permanent home
- location of your family, personal belongings, and automobile
- location of social, religious, cultural, and political organizations
- the bank where you conduct routine personal banking activities and investments and where you are registered to vote

"A Canadian should consider relying on the closer connection to a foreign country other than the U.S. as a last resort, since both the tax home and closer connection determinations may be subject to a degree of uncertainty. Keep in mind that this exception does not apply for any year during which you may have an application pending for adjustment to permanent resident status. Consult with a professional for guidance.

"To qualify for a closer connection exception to the Substantial Presence Test, you will need to file Form 8840, the Closer Connection Exception Statement for Aliens, with the IRS—the Internal Revenue Service—each year before June 15 for the previous calendar year. Filing Form 8840 in a timely matter is important; otherwise you could face myriad tax rules that could affect you adversely. If you file a U.S. income tax return, Form 1040NR, Form 8840 may be attached.

"If you do not file Form 8840 in a timely manner, this could cause the loss of your right to claim the exception for that tax year. The loss of this exception may cause you to be deemed a U.S. tax resident and therefore you would be required to file a U.S. 1040 tax return and declare your worldwide income. The purpose of filing Form 8840 is to advise the IRS that Canada is your tax home and that you maintained more significant ties to Canada than to the U.S. during the current year. If you are married or have children who also meet the Substantial Presence Test, each person is required to file Form 8840. Again, consulting with a cross-border professional is wise.

A Canadian may also rely on what's known as the treaty tie-breaker. Let's take a look at this, outlined in your handout."

- **Treaty tie-breaker**—Under the internal laws of both countries, you may be considered a resident of both Canada and the U.S. There is a Canada-U.S. Income Tax Convention (treaty) that can provide relief from being considered and taxed as a resident of both countries on your worldwide income. The treaty lists a number of criteria to determine your residency:

    a. First, you shall be deemed to be a resident solely of the country in which you have a permanent home available to you.

    b. If a permanent home is available to you in both countries or if a permanent home is not available in either country, you will be deemed to be a resident solely in the country in which your personal and economic relations are closer (what is known as your centre of vital interests).

c. If your centre of vital interests cannot be determined, you will be deemed to be a resident of the country in which you have a habitual abode.

d. If a habitual abode is available in both countries or in neither country, you will be deemed to be a resident of the country in which you are a citizen; or if you are a citizen of both countries or of neither, the competent authorities of the two countries will determine the query by mutual agreement.

Jonathan continued, "The intent of the treaty is to ensure an individual is not double taxed on the same income in Canada and the U.S. Be sure to consult with a cross-border professional; you want to ensure that you qualify to pass one of the above-described tests in favour of one country, so that you are protected from facing two sets of tax rules at the same time. Additionally, seek guidance from an immigration attorney if you hold a green card before claiming U.S. nonresident status, as it could jeopardize your U.S. immigration status.

"You'll need to file a nonresident U.S. federal income tax return (Form 1040NR) in order to claim the treaty tie-breaker provisions. Failure to file in a timely manner could result in penalties."

"I had no idea that we would need to count the number of days we spend in the U.S. and possibly file tax returns. At this stage in our careers, we're not able to spend more than 121 days annually in the U.S. But when we retire, we will need to be cognizant of this," said Eliza.

"This is important," replied Jonathan. "Many Canadians, especially snowbirds who spend the winter in the south, need to be aware of this. When you visit the U.S. for a vacation or perhaps as a snowbird, you enter the country on a temporary basis, as a visitor; you are not a resident. Generally, if you comply with the laws, you will be allowed to stay in the U.S. for up to 180 days annually.

"Remember, entry into the U.S. is a privilege, not a right. You are a visitor. If you wish to enjoy the warm weather and everything the U.S. has to offer, you need to be in compliance with U.S. laws. Filing the form is relatively simple. If you are deemed a U.S. resident for tax purposes and do not file the form, you may meet another set of U.S. tax filing and compliance issues and could be subject to penalties. You'll sleep better if you comply."

"I don't think our friends who purchased a Florida condo are aware of these rules," said Rob.

Terry commented, "Unfortunately, many Canadians are unaware of these and other rules."

Michelle said, "Just to confirm that I understand correctly, we are able to spend up to 180 days each year in the U.S. as a visitor. We should keep track of the number of days we spend in the U.S. and comply with filing the appropriate forms. And, with reference to the non-recourse mortgage, we should also consider the possibility of being exposed to U.S. estate tax for any real estate we may own in the U.S. Is that correct?"

"The Substantial Presence Test rules need to be followed, and you should keep track of the number of days annually that you spend in the U.S. You need to ensure that you adhere to the appropriate rules," replied Jonathan.

Terry stated, "Regarding U.S. estate planning, this is something you should investigate before acquiring a property. This topic may not be discussed during the purchase or closing process. Understand that, for the most part, real estate professionals, real estate lawyers, and title companies do not advise on this topic; this is not their specialty."

"I realize that I have given you a great deal of information today," said Jonathan. "I am not trying to overwhelm you, but you do need to be aware of the different laws and options with respect to purchasing a U.S. property. You are acquiring property in another country; there are rules and laws with which you need to comply. Being aware of these laws and rules and structuring yourself accordingly is an important consideration. The goal is for you to enjoy, as well as protect, your real estate investment."

CHAPTER 9

Ownership Options and Estate Planning

Terry thanked Jonathan for taking the group through the rules. Then she said, "Understanding how U.S. estate tax laws could impact your estate is important, as is compliance with the Substantial Presence Test rules and an awareness of titling options. Jonathan will now give us an overview of U.S. estate tax rules."

"And all you wanted to do was purchase a property to escape the winter and enhance your lifestyle! Well, the good news is that this is exactly what we want you to do; however, my goal is to also ensure that you understand how U.S. estate laws in particular could affect you and your loved ones, and to outline possible options to minimize or possibly eliminate estate tax," said Jonathan.

"Let me begin with some background on estate issues. If a Canadian citizen owns U.S. property, upon his or her death the property is called U.S. situs property. Why this is important is that U.S. situs property may be subject to U.S. estate tax on the full value of the property upon the death of the owner. U.S. estate taxes are expected to change in 2013. Property that is exposed to estate tax for Canadians who are nonresidents of the U.S. include real estate in the U.S.—land and buildings on the land; personal property such as cars, boats, furniture, and jewelry that is normally located in the U.S.; shares of U.S. corporations, even those held inside your RRSP or RRIFs; money market accounts with U.S. brokerages; and a golf club equity membership, among other items. However, U.S. bank deposits, term deposits and GICs, non-U.S. stocks, bonds and mutual funds, as well as real estate held outside the U.S. are not considered U.S. assets. It is important to understand what is exempt and what is included; exempt assets may be subject to probate."

Jonathan continued, "The Tax Relief, Unemployment Insurance Reauthorization, and Job Creation Act of 2010 was signed into law in December of that year, and it includes changes that affect U.S. gift and estate tax. U.S. estate tax is imposed on the *value* of the property, not on the *appreciation* of the property. Under the Internal Revenue Code, the estate of a non-U.S. resident noncitizen is allowed what is called a unified credit that exempts only $60,000 of U.S. situs property from U.S. state tax. Presently, if the value of your U.S. property is worth less than $60,000 when you pass away, there will be no U.S. estate tax. However, if the value of your U.S. property is greater than $60,000, there is a Canada-U.S. tax treaty that may qualify the estate for a greater exemption based on the formula outlined in the handout."

The Formula

$$\frac{\text{Unified credit exemption}}{\text{allowable to U.S. citizen}} \times \frac{\text{value of U.S. situs assets}}{\text{value of worldwide assets}}$$

"The unified credit allowable to a U.S. citizen exempts $5 million of assets from estate tax for 2012. When a spouse who owns the U.S. situs property dies and leaves it to a surviving spouse— assuming the couple is married—the exemption amount is in effect doubled because of a marital credit benefit. This means that in 2012, for Canadian couples with less than $10 million in worldwide assets, U.S. estate tax may be virtually eliminated at either spouse's death regardless of which spouse holds title," Jonathan continued.

"Understand, however, Canadians who are nonresidents and own assets such as real estate (land and buildings) may be exposed to U.S. tax. Consult with a cross-border professional for guidance on your individual situation.

"You will need to compare your total worldwide estate with your U.S. estate. The Canadian resident is not taxed on his or her worldwide estate, but only on U.S. assets, as long as the Canadian resident is not a U.S. citizen. However, the value of your worldwide estate is used to determine the rate you will be taxed on your U.S. assets. Generally speaking, the ratio of U.S. assets to worldwide assets is used to determine a Canadian resident's allowed exemption from U.S. estate tax, and a Canadian's nonresident exemption is equal to the pro rata amount that a U.S. citizen is allowed. Let's consider an example of a Canadian with a U.S. vacation property and other U.S. assets with a fair market value of US$400,000 and a worldwide net worth, including the U.S. vacation property, of US$2 million:

$$\frac{\text{value of U.S. situs assets} \;=\; \$400,000}{\text{value of worldwide assets} \;=\; \$2,000,000} \times \begin{array}{c}\$5.0\ \text{Million}\\ \text{exemption}\end{array}$$

"Given that the value of the worldwide estate, including the $400,000 property and other U.S. assets such as furniture, plus everything else owned anywhere in the world, is less than the $5-million exemption allowed in 2012, a person in this situation would not pay U.S. estate tax. That person may still be subject to Canadian deemed disposition tax upon death if his or her property and assets appreciated in value.

"Let's consider another example of a Canadian with a U.S. vacation property and other U.S. assets with a fair market value of US$1 million and a worldwide net worth of US$10 million:

$$\frac{\text{value of U.S. situs assets} = \$1,000,000}{\text{value of worldwide assets} = \$10,000,000} \times \begin{array}{c}\$5.0\ \text{Million}\\ \text{exemption}\end{array}$$

"In this example, 10 per cent of the deceased's assets are located in the U.S. This percentage is now applied to the available credit (equal to the tax on US$5 million), which results in a unified credit of approximately $173,080. As the estimated tax due is $330,800, this results in an estimated $157,720 of tax payable upon death (in 2012). With new tax laws likely due to come into effect in 2013 (as anticipated may be the case), the amount due would increase in 2013 if the $5-million exemption should decrease to $1 million, and the estate tax marginal rate may also increase.

"But if a married couple owned the property and the deceased left the U.S. assets to the surviving Canadian nonresident spouse, the unified credit may be doubled by a marital credit allowed under the Canada-U.S. tax treaty. That being the case, this would result in a unified credit of $173,080 and a marital credit amount of $173,080 (total of $346,160), which results in no estate tax due in 2012. Keep in mind that this would not be the case in 2013 if the worldwide exemption amount is decreased to US$1 million and the estate tax marginal rate increases as is anticipated. This would result in a significant difference!

"Another thing to keep in mind—a U.S. taxable estate also includes the value of life insurance policies that you own. In Canada, your life insurance policy proceeds are not usually taxable upon receipt, but the value of the insurance policy is normally included in your worldwide asset value. Thus, as an example, if you had a $1-million insurance policy, $1 million would be added to your worldwide estate's value. Some individuals consider creating a life insurance trust to own their policies; this keeps the proceeds of the life insurance policy out of the estate but allows designated trustees to distribute the proceeds according to the policy holder's written instructions.

"Pensions are another consideration—your U.S. taxable estate also includes the present value of all the future payments you may leave to a spouse under any spousal benefit of your pension. And the value of a Canadian-controlled private corporation that you control or have controlled and in which you still own shares.

"In Canada, the deemed disposition tax on appreciated assets upon death is in effect an income tax on capital gains. Generally, since the U.S. estate tax is not an income tax, the Canadian Revenue Agency, or CRA, does not allow a foreign tax credit on estate tax paid to the U.S. to offset the Canadian deemed disposition tax. Conversely, the IRS does not allow any deemed disposition tax paid to the CRA as a credit against U.S. estate taxes payable," said Jonathan.

"Does this mean we are double taxed?" asked Cathy.

"That's exactly where I am going," replied Jonathan. "Think about this: Canadians who own U.S. real estate that has appreciated in value may face two separate taxes on the same assets at the same time without obtaining offsetting credits. The Canada-U.S. treaty may allow you to receive a partial credit that helps to reduce your estate tax liability. Calculating the amount of estate tax you may owe is a complicated formula. There are also a few estate planning strategies Canadians can use to legally minimize U.S. nonresident estate tax. As you can see, it's prudent to consult with an experienced cross-border professional to determine an appropriate strategy favourable to your individual circumstances.

"One other very important item to consider is how to take title to the U.S. property, whether that be individually in the name of one spouse only, or in both spouses' names as tenants in common or joint tenants—and they are different—or perhaps through a trust or other entity.

"Property that is owned jointly with rights of survivorship (as is a common ownership structure in Canada) or community property with rights of survivorship is common for married couples. The U.S. may not recognize common-law marriage the same as Canada does, and rights of spouses differ between these two types of ownership; consult an attorney for advice on differences. With some types of ownership, the property passes automatically to the surviving spouse, avoiding probate—but be careful and seek legal advice from a cross-border professional, as this may lead to U.S. estate tax in each spouse's estate with no ability to mitigate the taxes owed through wills because the property may have, by operation of law, passed to the surviving spouse. Estate tax rates are graduated and rose to 35 per cent in 2011. In 2013, assuming the laws change, the maximum tax rate on U.S. assets is anticipated to increase to 55 per cent.

"For non-U.S. residents, the presumption may be that the first spouse to die contributed all the funds, despite joint ownership of the property, and the entire value of the property—not half—could be included in the descendant's estate on the death of the first spouse, and then it will be included again when the surviving spouse dies. This could be the case unless you can successfully prove that the property was funded from two separate bank accounts and that each party paid half or that the entire amount was funded by the surviving spouse. Be prepared to show proof.

"At present, the Canada-U.S. treaty provides some relief for Canadians. Remember, tax acts and laws can change; the unknown is when and how this could affect you. It is important for you to properly plan and structure how you title the property beforehand, as there may be tax consequences for changing your options after you purchase the property. Laws also may be different for a Canadian citizen who is a green card holder.

"The estate of a deceased person is administered, and all claims and distribution of the deceased's property under a will is done by a legal process known as probate. Probate can be expensive and time-consuming. Strategies and options exist to avoid probate. If you are planning to open a U.S. bank account in America, consider setting up the U.S. bank account with P.O.D. (meaning 'paid on death')."

Titling Options

Jonathan paused to allow everyone to review and grasp the material before continuing. "Now let's discuss titling options. You have options of how to structure ownership; each option has pros and cons to consider and every buyer's decision of which route to select will be based on each personal situation. There is no standard one solution that fits all; it depends on each buyer's individual circumstances. It is wise to consult with a knowledgeable cross-border professional to discuss your goals and options and to assist you with determining the appropriate solution for your needs. This is an important decision; take the time to become educated and consult a cross-border professional for assistance.

"Let's look at a summary of your options. In general terms, you either title real estate through individual names, which is not limited to two people, or through an entity. States have different types of property ownership; generally, two types of laws to own property exist—either common-law states or community property law states. Take a look at the list in your handout."

1. **Joint tenancy (with right of survivorship)**—This occurs when a property is titled in individual names as joint tenants. This is a common way for couples to own Canadian real estate; the surviving person (spouse or other person) becomes the owner. Probate is avoided upon the death of the first owner but not on the death of the second. Should you become incapacitated and the property needed to be sold, a time-consuming and expensive guardianship procedure may be necessary—consider having durable power of attorney set up. Seek cross-border professional advice.

   Currently, each individual nonresident has a $60,000 U.S. estate tax exemption and possibly more under the Canada-U.S. treaty. If one of the owners dies, the IRS may assume that the first to die has contributed all of the capital for the purchase of the property. The end result is that the entire value of the U.S. property could be included in the estate of the first person to die unless the executor can prove that the surviving spouse contributed funds toward the purchase of the property. As there is right of survivorship associated with joint tenancy, it does not allow for any will planning.

2. **Tenants in common (ownership without right of survivorship)**—This form of ownership allows all owners to structure their last will and testaments as they wish to protect their interests. The property does not transfer automatically upon death, and there is probate upon death. There is the

possibility of an expensive and time-consuming guardian-ship process should an owner become incapacitated and the property needs to be sold. There may be multiple owners, and ownership can be in unequal percentages. U.S. estate tax still applies.

3. **Tenancy by the entirety**—The surviving spouse owns the property and probate is avoided, similar to joint tenancy. With this form of ownership, each tenant owns the entire estate and neither can sell or convey his or her interest inde-pendent of the other. U.S. estate tax still applies.

4. **Community property (without the right of survivor-ship)**—Each spouse of a married couple owns a half-interest in the property and may pass his or her ownership interest by will on death. Probate is not avoided, and U.S. estate tax still applies.

5. **Community property (with the right of survivorship)**—Each spouse of a married couple owns a half-interest in the property, and if one owner dies, the survivor owns the prop-erty. Probate is avoided upon the death of the first owner. U.S. estate tax still applies.

Note: The U.S. may not recognize common-law marriage the same as Canada does; if you are not legally married accord-ing to U.S. law, estate tax and other laws may be difficult. It is prudent to consult with a cross-border professional.

6. **Individual name**—You hold title, own and control the property. There will be probate on death, and U.S. estate tax applies. Also, if you become incapacitated and require a guardianship procedure, this can be time-consuming and expensive. There is no tax-free rollover or right of survivor-ship to a surviving spouse.

7. **Own the property with your children**—Your adult chil-dren and you are co-owners as joint tenants with the right of survivorship. This does avoid probate if the parents die first; however, a time-consuming and expensive guardian

procedure may be required if one of the co-owners becomes incapacitated and the property needs to be sold. Also, the property could be exposed to seizure if one of the co-owners (for example, any of the adult children) has financial problems.

Note: Seek legal advice regarding adding children to title unless they are contributing funds, as you may be exposed to U.S. gift tax. U.S. estate tax still applies. Again, laws in the U.S. are different from those in Canada—it is important for you to consult with a cross-border specialist.

8. **Canadian corporation**—In this case, a Canadian corporation holds title to the U.S. property in order to avoid direct ownership. This entity avoids probate and incapacity issues. For U.S. estate tax purposes, there could be an issue whether the IRS will respect the corporation as the true owner of the property; it may ignore the corporation for estate tax purposes and the shareholder could be exposed to U.S. estate tax regardless of the corporate ownership of the property. Tax obligations in Canada and the U.S. should be considered. Professional guidance from a cross-border estate attorney and a cross-border accountant is prudent prior to implementing this strategy.

9. **Nonrecourse mortgage**—A type of mortgage whereby the only security is the actual property. If there is a default of the mortgage, the property is the only asset that the lender can go after. The lender cannot go after any of your other assets. Of course, this would affect your credit rating. A nonrecourse mortgage has the advantage of being deductible from your taxable estate (dollar for dollar), with only the net equity being taxable. Keep in mind that not all debt is subtracted when determining a taxable estate—only nonrecourse debt is. There are a few U.S. lenders, including Canadian subsidiary banks in the U.S., that may provide a nonrecourse mortgage. (More on lender nonrecourse mortgages later.)

10. **Life insurance**—You could title the property to your own individual name(s) and then purchase term life insurance in sufficient value to cover any possible estate tax. This would incur a monthly cost, and the older you are, the more expensive the insurance. Thus, you need to weigh the cost versus the benefit. In Canada, upon death, there is usually no tax on life insurance; however, in the U.S., life insurance is included as part of your worldwide estate for U.S. estate tax purposes (unless a separate life insurance trust is created to own the insurance policies).

11. **Limited partnership and limited liability partnership**—These are two types of partnerships. Depending on the value of the property and the owner's worldwide net worth, the use of the property (vacation or investment property) and objectives of the partners, this structure may be combined with other entities. This is a sophisticated structure, may be expensive to set up, and may have annual reporting requirements. Seek advice from cross-border legal and tax professionals.

12. **Trust (irrevocable)**—Once created, an irrevocable trust cannot be changed to be set up as a cross-border strategy. It may eliminate the imposition of U.S. estate tax upon the death of either spouse, as well as provide creditor protection features. The entity may also have income tax advantages if the property is sold, as it may allow the long-term capital gains rates for a property owned more than one year. Appropriate wording for the trust is important. Currently, U.S. rates are 15 per cent federally (properties owned for a minimum of 12 months), whereas the ordinary income and short-term capital gains rates for individuals are at a maximum rate of 35 per cent federally.

   Canadians are still required to file a Canadian tax return upon the sale of U.S. property and report any capital gains. If any U.S. capital gains tax is due and paid to the IRS, this would create a foreign tax credit that could be applied to the Canadian tax return to offset some of the Canadian capital gains tax due.

Important rules exist on the use of a trust that must be followed, which include funding of the trust for the purchase and closing, control, and observation of Canada's 21-year rule for distribution. What this means is that the property in the trust is deemed to have been sold at fair market value every 21 years, and the gain or loss is reported on the trust tax return. In addition, some trusts are considered flow-through entities and do not protect you from estate tax. Generally, an individual who creates an irrevocable trust may have no rights or control once the trust is established. It is important that you discuss this with a knowledgeable cross-border tax professional.

The trust should be set up before purchasing a U.S. property, and your contract of purchase and sale, along with the closing paperwork and ideally a bank account, should be in the name of the trust.

13. **Trust (revocable)**—There are several types of trusts. This special type of structure may avoid probate and incapacity and guardianship issues. With this type of trust, the trust owner is the grantor, trustee, and beneficiary of his or her trust, and a spouse can be a co-trustee. If there is no income on the property, then no annual filings or other legal work need to be done annually. This trust can be revoked or amended during the owner's lifetime and allows the owner to control who inherits his or her interest. If the property is being used as a rental (income) property, consider personal liability solutions, as this entity does not provide liability protection. (See Chapter 13 for more details.)

If you purchase and title U.S. property in an individual name and then transfer the property into a trust afterward, depending on the type of trust, this could raise U.S. gift, income, or tax issues, which may be costly. It is important to consult with an experienced cross-border attorney before implementing any strategies.

Jonathan continued, "There are a number of items you need to understand in order to decide on the best strategy or strategies for you. Many states have legislated their own separate estate tax. Others levy an annual personal property tax. Individual states are not bound by the Canada-U.S. tax treaty, and a nonresident could face a new source of tax at the state level without any treaty protection. Potential incapacity issues also need to be considered; perhaps consider having a durable power of attorney in place. It is important for you to consider the estate, tax, and legal issues and consult with a cross-border professional.

"It will be important to know which states may implement a state estate tax and plan around them accordingly. As an example, Arizona, California, and Florida have no state estate tax. As all states in the U.S. are currently facing budget deficits, you may expect for them to be looking to raise more money from their residents and property owners. In addition, a few states allow property to be transferred on death to the beneficiary by way of a beneficiary deed. Laws vary from state to state.

"Purchasing a U.S. vacation or retirement property is a lifestyle enhancement, but remember, it is also an asset and investment. If you are considering purchasing U.S. investment property for rental purposes, you may require different insurance (including liability coverage), asset protection, and legal or tax advice. In addition to estate, legal, and tax considerations, you also want to consider asset-protection strategies. Cross-border professional legal, tax, insurance, and asset protection advice and planning are important. It is prudent for you to consult with cross-border legal professionals, including a cross-border accountant and insurance professional, and possibly also a mortgage professional as well as a cross-border financial planner to review and determine the best course of action based on your worldwide financial assets and short- and long-term financial goals.

"Try not to feel overwhelmed by all of these considerations. Estate, tax, legal, insurance, and finance considerations all require professional advice—which is eminently available. You also need to understand what types of protection you are getting—or not getting—and your options. Are you considering protection from probate and minimizing estate tax exposure, or are you focusing on asset protection? Sometimes, provisions you want to put in place for one issue, say, an estate plan, may have little or no effect on another issue such as creditor protection, which may require different strategies. There is no one-size-fits-all solution; individual professional advice for your specific circumstances is important.

"You are also responsible for filing appropriate and timely tax returns; ignorance is no excuse. It is important to understand all your options and responsibilities."

"This information is fantastic; it would never have occurred to me to ask questions about estate planning or titling of real estate, or asset protection and taxes. I would have assumed that it was the same as here in Canada," commented Eliza.

Cathy agreed. "I wouldn't have known to ask about these things. Like Rob mentioned, I don't think our friends who recently purchased a Florida condo know this depth of information."

Terry said, "It's likely the case that many Canadian buyers are not aware of these issues. I say this because I have heard of people who seek legal advice after they have purchased U.S. property and have run into a residency, tax, or unfortunate estate situation."

"Terry, I understand why you emphasize a systematic, objective-oriented plan," said Mary. "I don't know *what* I don't know. Does the program provide checklists and names of cross-border professionals?"

"Rest assured, the program includes checklists of several steps and issues Canadian buyers of U.S. real estate should understand so that you can make careful decisions during the buying and closing process. Now, there are a few more items that I would like to cover before we wrap up for the night. Let's review the details of an irrevocable and revocable trust," said Jonathan.

CHAPTER 10

Nonresident Estate Planning

Trust (Irrevocable)

Jonathan asked the group to turn to the section in their handouts titled "Trusts," then continued, "As we have discussed, one of the options or strategies to consider for dealing with U.S. estate tax is to have a trust created. There are a number of different types of trusts, but let's focus on a version of an irrevocable trust. As an example, let's consider a married couple with children whose worldwide net worth is in excess of $10 million. In this case, they may want to consider an irrevocable trust, specifically worded, which would avoid the imposition of U.S. estate tax at the death of either spouse while also providing creditor protection features.

"In utilizing this type of trust, one spouse would be the settlor/grantor of the trust and contribute all the funds toward the purchase of the property. The trust would be for the benefit of the grantor's spouse and any descendants they wish to be a beneficiary. The trust would acquire the property.

"The trustee could be either the grantor's spouse—who also could be a beneficiary—or an independent friend or third party. They may decide to have a successor trustee; however, the settlor/grantor could not be the trustee. The beneficiaries of the trust have lifetime rent-free use of the property, and distributions from the trust could be made to the beneficiaries for health, education, maintenance, and support."

Jonathan went on to explain that the trust should be created and signed before making an offer to purchase, as the contract of purchase and closing paperwork, including title to the property, need to be in the name of the trust. The trust or the beneficiary spouse would pay the maintenance expenses associated with the property. Unless the trust had U.S. source income—that is, rental income—or until the property is sold, there is no requirement for the trust to file a U.S. tax return for the property.

"Appropriate wording needs to be included in the trust to ensure it is set up as a cross-border strategy; otherwise, this could be an issue. It is important to understand the rules involved in using this type of trust. Ask a cross-border attorney for specific wording and setup of the appropriate trust," explained Jonathan.

"As you can see, cross-border tax and estate law is a specialty that requires professional advice," Terry commented.

Lindsey added, "I would never have known about estate, residency, taxes, and these other laws and considerations. Thankfully, we have this information and understand the need to seek appropriate professional guidance before acquiring a U.S. property."

Cathy asked, "You mentioned that this trust is irrevocable—what does that mean?"

"Good question," Jonathan replied. "It means that once it is created, it cannot be amended. Which brings me to another option. Sometimes instead of an irrevocable trust, and for a variety of reasons, a *revocable trust* is created. This is a different strategy."

Trust (Revocable)

Jonathan continued, "For example, earlier this week, a revocable trust—with cross-border wording—was created for a couple who have been together for 15 years and in Canada are considered common-law spouses. This was done based on several factors such as their world-wide net worth; the price they planned to spend on a U.S. property; and the likelihood that the U.S. may not recognize common-law spouses in the same way that Canada recognizes them—and there were a few other issues, too. With this strategy, each person will have his or her own trust, and each trust will hold a 50-per-cent ownership of the property. Individually, they are the grantor, trustee, and beneficiary of their separate trusts, and they are co-trustees of each other's trust. This type of trust can be revoked or amended, and there is no annual tax filing unless there is rental income, nor any legal work to complete on an annual basis. In addition, this type of trust may avoid probate, as trusts do not die; and also, this strategy avoids expensive and time-consuming guardianship processes if one becomes mentally incapacitated."

Terry commented, "Sounds like there are different options depending on the needs and circumstances of the individuals involved."

Jonathan said, "Since the separate trusts each own 50 per cent, the U.S. taxable estate is reduced in half upon each person's death. If the couple chose to title the property together jointly with a right of survivorship, it may be possible to avoid probate on the death of the first person. Now the survivor owns the property outright and can do whatever he or she wishes with it, including naming family members as beneficiaries. However, probate will be required at the death of the second person. It may also be possible for the estates to use valuation discounts to further reduce the value of the asset, which also lowers the tax."

"Valuation discounts—how does that work?" asked Terry.

"The U.S. definition of fair market value is the price that a willing buyer and seller would agree on if both have reasonable knowledge or relevant facts and neither are compelled to buy or sell. Several factors could influence what a willing and knowledgeable buyer would pay. For example, many buyers would not pay the same price for a property over which they lack control or liquidity, as there are restrictions, and, therefore, they would likely value it lower," replied Jonathan.

"Therefore, if the two trusts each own a 50 per cent interest, and one trust attempted to sell its 50 per cent interest on the open market, it could be difficult to find a buyer willing to pay 50 per cent of the fair market value of the whole property. Acceptable valuation discounts allowed by the IRS range from 20 to 33 per cent. Consider this example:"

Fair market value of the property	$600,000
50-per-cent ownership interest	$300,000
Valuation discount of 20 per cent	$60,000
U.S. estate ($300,000 minus $60,000)	$240,000

"So, by using two separate trusts as you described, each with a 50-per cent ownership interest in the property, using the valuation discounts could further reduce the taxable estate amount?" questioned Terry.

Jonathan said, "That's correct. It may also be possible to defer any tax owed if a tax-free rollover provision—which is special wording that is included in this trust—exists; there would be no U.S. tax payable upon the death of the first person."

"Thank you, Jonathan," Terry said. "This is certainly specialized knowledge and you have explained some important options."

"We've covered an overview of several options and, as you can see, there is no one-size-fits-all solution. Each situation is different, and there are different strategies depending on many factors," responded Jonathan.

"Thank you, Jonathan, Diana, and Terry," Cathy said. "I am sure that I speak for the group. I'm glad that we have had this opportunity to participate in these meetings and am grateful for the information you've all presented. I feel more comfortable moving forward with our purchase plans."

Terry smiled and said, "We are fortunate that our guests have graciously joined us and shared this important information. It is important that before investing, whether you are purchasing a vacation or investment/rental property, you understand and assess the different cross-border estate, tax, and legal obligations and rules that exist; seek advice from cross-border professionals."

Laura asked, looking at Jonathan, "I realize that I will need to set up an individual meeting with you to review my own situation; however, my question relates to renting the property. I assume there are rules for rental income tax—can you offer any information about this?"

Jonathan turned to Diana, saying, "This is your specialty— Diana, why don't you take over from here?"

Note: There are many types of trusts for different purposes and to meet individual needs. David A. Altro, managing partner at Altro & Associates, LLP created the Cross-Border Trust^{SM}. Proper and appropriate wording is necessary for a trust to be effective. Refer to David's book *Owning U.S. Property - The Canadian Way* (rapidBOOKS, 2011). Always seek experienced cross-border professional advice.

CHAPTER 11

What You Need to Know about Tax Filings, Gains, and Foreign Tax Credits

Diana said, "I'm impressed by the calibre of questions this group is asking, and I commend you all for taking the time to educate yourselves on potential tax and other responsibilities.

"If it is your intention to receive rental income from your property by renting it, whether it be on a part-time or full-time basis, you are required to file U.S. income tax returns and report the rental income. Depending on the state in which the property is located, you may be required to pay both state and federal tax on the income. State and local tax rules may vary depending on the jurisdiction. Some cities and counties may also impose sales tax on rental properties. There are many possibilities; specialized local knowledge is important. It is important that you consult with a tax professional and become aware of all the potential tax liabilities."

"Excuse me, Diana, but I have heard that Canadians need to declare rental income in the U.S. as well as in Canada. Does this mean we'd be taxed twice?" asked Lindsey.

"Well, generally you are required to report rental income by filing U.S. and Canadian tax returns. Some countries allow tax credits against income that was also taxed in another country. I believe that the Canada-U.S. tax treaty allows you to claim a foreign tax credit on your Canadian return, so be sure to check with your Canadian tax advisor about this," answered Diana.

Flat Tax, or Trade or Business Tax

"When renting property in the U.S., you have two options," Diana continued. "The first option is a 30-per-cent nonresident withholding tax assessed on the gross rent. This can be deducted by your property manager, if you are using one, or by the tenant. This amount is remitted to the IRS. This is known as a flat tax. Keep in mind that with this there are no deductions for expenses."

The room was silent as the group absorbed this information. Diana continued, "The second option is that the IRS permits you to pay tax on the net income after deductible expenses, which may result in less tax owed. Your property and any rental income could be considered a U.S. trade or business, and you may be able to claim deductions such as property tax, utilities, insurance, mortgage interest, maintenance, and depreciation. The result normally is a lower taxable amount, if any. You would be required to file a nonresident tax return.

"Be careful about mortgage interest, as the IRS permits mortgage interest as a deduction so long as the mortgage is secured by the rented property.

"If you wish to set up your rental to be exempt from the 30-per-cent withholding tax at source, you will need to obtain a U.S. individual taxpayer identification number, or ITIN, and file Form W-8ECI with your rental agent. You will also be required to file Form 1040NR each year in which you have any rental income. It is very important to obtain tax advice from a cross-border professional and understand your obligations. You need to ensure that you file your U.S. return in a timely manner; failure to file by the due date could subject you to the 30-per-cent tax on the gross rental income, with no allowance for any deductions or expenses.

"Don't assume that because your expenses exceeded the rental income that you need not bother filing a tax return. You are still required to file in the U.S.," emphasized Diana.

"This is important," Eliza said. "If I decide to rent out the home on a part-time basis to offset some of the annual expenses, even if the income is lower than the allowed deductible expenses, thereby offsetting any tax owing, am I still required to file a U.S. tax return?"

"Yes, especially if you don't want to pay a flat 30-per-cent non-resident withholding tax and at least have the ability to deduct allowable expenses. If you don't file, even if there is no tax payable, you may be forced to pay tax and penalties on the gross rent collected, thus costing you more money," replied Diana.

Canadian Tax Filing

"You are also required to report any net rental income on your Canadian tax return, currency adjusted for Canadian dollars," advised Diana. "You take any tax paid in the U.S. as a foreign tax credit on your Canadian return. The U.S. and Canada may have different rates for depreciation and for wear and tear on the property.

"Consult with an accountant or lawyer with experience in cross-border taxation. This professional can provide guidance and advice to minimize, if not eliminate, tax and ensure that the appropriate forms are filed in a timely and correct manner."

"Would we be required to set up a U.S. dollar account in the U.S. to deposit the rental income?" asked Laura.

"You can do this, though it's not mandatory," said Diana. "A nonresident who is required to file a U.S. tax return will need to get an ITIN, the taxpayer's identification number. It's like a social insurance number in Canada.

"You apply for the ITIN by completing IRS Form W-7, or have your accountant or lawyer do this for you. If you use an accountant or lawyer to do this, consider finding one that is an IRS-certified Acceptance Agent. The IRS has stopped routinely issuing ITINs—you must prove that you need one. An Acceptance Agent not only can help with the numerous rules for this application but also may be able to obtain the number faster than if you apply by yourself. You cannot apply for this number at the U.S. Social Security Administration offices, nor is this something that can be obtained in just a few days.

"The ITIN needs to be supplied to your rental agent to prevent the 30-per-cent withholding tax and needs to go on your U.S. tax return. If you should decide to open an interest-bearing U.S. bank account, the bank may also ask for this ITIN.

"You can have a U.S. dollar account in Canada and deposit rental income there as well. For convenience purposes, many people with a U.S. mortgage open a U.S. bank account and transfer funds into this account every month to pay their mortgage. They use this U.S. bank account for all U.S. house-related income and expenses," explained Diana.

"Again, it's important to note that tax laws are different in Canada from the U.S. Additionally, laws vary from state to state. Items that are deductible in one country or state may or may not be deductible in the other. Consult with the appropriate tax or legal professionals to be sure."

Sale of U.S. Real Estate

"If you sell your U.S. property, whether or not you have chosen to rent the property during your ownership, you will need to file a U.S. tax return and report any gain or loss on Form 1040NR—the U.S. nonresident alien income tax return. You pay U.S. federal tax on any capital gains. In addition, you will need to report any capital gains of your U.S. property on your Canadian tax return," Diana advised.

"As a Canadian, you need to be aware that when you sell your U.S. property, 10 per cent of the gross sales price is withheld and due under FIRPTA, the Foreign Investment in Real Property Tax Act of 1980. This 10-per-cent withholding tax is offset against the U.S. income tax that is due on capital gains. If the 10-per-cent withholding exceeds the tax liability, a refund is sent to you. It is the buyer's responsibility to withhold 10 per cent of the gross purchase price and pay it to the IRS. If the buyer fails to withhold the 10 per cent and pay it to the IRS, the

IRS may assess the 10 per cent against the buyer. However, there are two exceptions to reduce or eliminate the 10-per-cent withholding, as outlined in the handout."

Withholding Exceptions

1. **Sales price is less than $300,000.** One exception is that an individual buyer does not have to withhold the 10 per cent when the purchase price does not exceed $300,000 and he or she has definite plans to use the property as a residence during each of the first two 12-month periods immediately after acquisition. The term "residence" is a technical term. An individual purchaser satisfies the residency test if the buyer or members of his or her family reside at the property at least 50 per cent of the number of days that it is used by any person during each of the first two 12-month periods immediately after the purchase. Check with the IRS or your accountant (CPA) for additional information.

   A Canadian individual buyer should not rely on the exception when purchasing from a foreign seller unless he/she is absolutely sure that he/she is not going to rent the property for more than an insignificant amount of time during the first two years that he/she owns the property. It is the buyer who takes on all the risk and gets nothing in return when he/she relies on this exception. By relying on this exception, buyers are giving up their right to change their mind and rent the property for the majority of time during these two 12-month periods. If a buyer is not sure, he or she should withhold the 10 per cent from the purchase price and pay it to the IRS or have the foreign seller apply for relief from the 10-per-cent withholding tax from the IRS. It is in the buyer's best interest to seek professional advice when faced with this situation.

   If you are selling, consider having the buyer sign a specific schedule outlining his or her intentions to utilize the property. Many state real estate boards have preprinted

forms for this purpose. The seller is still required to file a
U.S. tax return and pay tax on any capital gains in a timely
manner.

If tax is due on this transaction, you may be subject to
underpayment penalties if no tax is withheld on closing.

---

2. **Withholding certificate.** You can apply for a withholding
   certificate from the IRS. If you expect that the tax due will be
   less than the 10 per cent withholding, you can apply before
   the closing date for this certificate. You need to file Form 8288
   (Application for Withholding Certificate for Dispositions
   by Foreign Persons of U.S. Real Estate Property Interests).
   Form 8288 is a detailed tax calculation that demonstrates to
   the IRS the amount of gain or loss on the specific real estate
   transaction. A separate Form 8288 is required for each sale of
   real property. The IRS usually takes approximately 90 days to
   make this determination and send a response.

   When you receive your certificate, it will indicate what
   the tax amount will be, and that is the amount that will be
   withheld. If you receive the certificate after the closing of the
   property, the full 10 per cent would have been withheld at
   closing—usually by the closing agent or attorney. On the
   IRS certificate, the amount of the withholding that should
   be returned to you will be stated with the remainder (if any)
   going directly to the IRS.

   Regardless of whether you opted to reduce or eliminate
   the withholding on the sale of the real property, the gross
   amount of the sale is reported to the IRS on Form 1099-S,
   and your net gain or loss must be reported to the IRS on
   Form 1040NR, which is due by June 15 of the year following the transaction. Any withholding sent to the IRS is also
   reported to the IRS via Form 8288. A copy of these forms
   should be provided to you so that you can prove to the IRS
   any funds withheld.

You will be able to claim tax withheld for FIRPTA purposes on your tax return. You will also need to report the capital gains of the U.S. sale on your Canadian return. If you have been a resident of Canada before September 27, 1980, you will likely be able to enjoy the Canada-U.S. tax treaty benefit to reduce the gain that has accrued since January 1, 1985, or later. U.S. tax paid allows you to claim a foreign tax credit to reduce Canadian tax on the sale.

Diana continued, "On the sale of the U.S. property, the application for reduced withholding should be sent to the IRS as soon as possible once you have a signed sales contract. It could take eight to 12 weeks or more for you to receive a withholding certificate. You will also be required to obtain an ITIN if you have not previously done so by filing Form W-7 and you need to include this with your Form 8288 submission.

"Please do not confuse an exemption from withholding tax with an exemption to pay tax. Consider the 10-per-cent withholding tax as an estimated tax payment. If there is a gain, tax is owed; it just may be less (or more) than the 10-per-cent withholding amount. In addition, some states have a state income tax. Seek advice from a tax or legal professional experienced with cross-border taxation for your Canadian tax return, and a certified public accountant in the U.S. who specializes in the international arena. Proper planning and professional assistance can reduce and in some cases eliminate tax."

"This certainly is a great deal of valuable information, Diana," said Terry.

Diana said, "I agree that this is a great deal of information to digest and think about. I simply want to give you an overview of the responsibilities Canadian buyers have. My objective is to navigate you through the tax rules, which can change over time."

"I feel so much more comfortable and knowledgeable about stepping into ownership of U.S. property now. A month ago I felt bewildered and nervous, and didn't know where to start and whom to contact," said Helen.

Diana responded, "The number of Canadian buyers this last year has increased for our firm. Several factors, such as the strength of the Canadian dollar, low interest rates, and the decline in real estate prices have presented Canadian buyers with an opportunity."

"This is precisely why we are so interested. Thank you, Diana," replied Mary.

Terry stepped in. "Can you believe we have been here for two and a half hours tonight? Time flies. I think we should let our guests get back to their families; however, they have included their contact information with their packages. Feel free to consult with them regarding your specific situation. Just before we pack up and head out, to summarize, let's review a checklist of items for you to consider. I know there are a number of items that we have yet to cover, but this will at least give you a glance at the big picture."

PURCHASE PROGRAM CHECKLIST

1. Budget
   - Down payment available?
   - Obtain mortgage preapproval and determine purchase price.
   - Obtain financing from Canadian or U.S. lender.
   - Set closing costs budget.
   - Budget to visit U.S. city to review property—airfare, accommodations, and out-of-pocket expenses.
   - U.S. medical/health care insurance costs and eligibility for health insurance coverage.
2. Location
   - Determine state/city and general neighbourhood.
3. Property utilization
   - Consider if property is personal use or rental property.

   Note: This may impact title considerations, structure, and source of financing.

4. Estate planning specialist
   - Speak with cross-border professional to determine and set up entity where applicable (e.g., titling, financing, insurance).

5. Search and view
   - Determine type of property, and needs and wants in property and community (Property Profile).
   - Speak with a U.S. real estate professional.
   - Become educated on real estate options and market.
   - View properties and areas.

6. Offer to purchase
   - Review comparative sold data with real estate professional.
   - Review offer and determine your strategy.
   - Negotiate offer with seller.
   - Sign offer.

7. Satisfaction of conditions
   - Submit escrow deposit and paperwork to closing agent and/or attorney.
   - Provide lender with purchase agreement for approval (where applicable).
   - Conduct applicable inspections and appraisals.
   - Requisition applicable HOA and estoppel/status documents.

8. Removal of conditions and title work
   - Remove conditions once satisfied.
   - Arrange for closing and initial transfer of funds.

9. Insurance
   - Set up property and third-party liability insurance (ideally during the conditional time period).
   - Arrange medical insurance.

10. Closing

    - Review documents.

    - Arrange wire transfer of funds for closing.

    - Attend closing—sign applicable documents and obtain keys.

    Note: Arrangements may be made to close transaction while you are in Canada—speak to the closing agent, attorney, or real estate professional to arrange.

11. Keep track of time spent in the U.S.

    - Keep log of number of days spent in the U.S. (annually).

12. Certified public accountant

    - Consult with a cross-border accounting/tax specialist, especially if you are spending more than 121 days annually in the U.S. and are receiving rental income.

Diana added, "If you're planning to rent your property, there are more rules and requirements to comply with. Regarding rental income, certain expense deductions are applicable, as are estate planning, insurance, and financing considerations. We have covered enough information to give you a framework to begin your own plan."

Cathy said, "From my perspective, we have completed the process of mortgage financing and determining our budget, and the professionals Terry introduced to us have been excellent. Rob and I feel comfortable and confident with the process and in control; this is a great feeling."

Terry smiled. "Your feedback is important; I'm pleased to hear the information and resources are helpful."

As the participants began to gather up their belongings, a few couples approached Terry to tell her that they wished to set up private meetings to discuss how to begin their own program.

CHAPTER 12

You're Prepared and Ready to Buy: Now What?

A few weeks later, Terry received a call from Cathy and Rob. "Hi, Terry. We're calling from Orlando, and we just had a great day! Nina, the real estate broker you introduced us to, is fantastic. We just wanted to let you know how things are going." Cathy could barely contain her enthusiasm. "We viewed nine properties in four different communities today and are viewing more tomorrow."

"Well done!" exclaimed Terry. "And I'm pleased to hear that you like Nina. I've worked with her several times, always with great results and positive feedback. Have you narrowed your search down to any specific community or area?"

"Yes, we really like a community just west of what is called the chain of lakes. We viewed a house today that is now on our short list. Nina is showing us another house or two in the same community tomorrow, as well as a few more communities. She is so well organized—and there were no bad surprises. We even felt like we knew where we were going. The information package Nina couriered to us, along with the Internet information she sent beforehand, helped us navigate the city. Rob and I feel very comfortable," said Cathy.

PROPERTY CHECKLIST

Property Address: _____

List Price: $ _____ Days on Market: _____

Other Information: _____

Date Viewed: _____

Property Age: _____ Brand New Construction: _____ Resale: _____ Builder: _____

Community Name: _____

Type: Freehold: _____ Condo: _____ Other: _____

      Detached: _____ Semi-detached: _____ Townhouse: _____ Link: _____ Duplex: _____

      Condominium Apartment: _____ Other: _____

Property Taxes: $ _____ Condominium Fees: $ _____

HOA: $ _____ Other: $ _____

Lot Size: _____

Waterfront: Yes: _____ No: _____ Details: _____

Community or HOA Name: _____

Community or HOA: Guard Gated: Yes: _____ No: _____ Other Details: _____

HOA Fee: $ _____ Paid: Monthly: _____ Quarterly: _____ Annually: _____ HOA Fee Includes: _____

Community Amenities:				
Pool:	Yes: ___ No: ___	Country Club:	Yes: ___ No: ___	
Restaurant/Dining:	Yes: ___ No: ___	Tennis:	Yes: ___ No: ___	
Gym/Fitness:	Yes: ___ No: ___	Library:	Yes: ___ No: ___	
Children's Playground:	Yes: ___ No: ___	Meeting Room:	Yes: ___ No: ___	
Boat Launch:	Yes: ___ No: ___	Marina/Boat Storage:	Yes: ___ No: ___	

Lake/Water Details: _____

Other: _____

Is there an HOA? Yes: _____ No: _____ Is membership mandatory? Yes: _____ No: _____

HOA Membership Details: _____

Golf Course: Yes: _____ No: _____ Golf Course Initiation Fee: $ _____

Golf Course Dues: $ _____ Paid: Monthly: _____ Quarterly: _____ Annual: _____

Golf Membership Details: _____

Golf Membership Approval Required: Yes: _____ No: _____ Details: _____

Social Membership: Yes: _____ No: _____ Is Social Membership Mandatory? Yes: _____ No: _____

Social Membership Initiation Fee: $ _____

Social Membership Ongoing Fee: $ _____ Paid: Monthly: _____ Quarterly: _____ Annual: _____

Social Membership Details: _____

HOA/Community Comments: _____

_____

_____

Condominium: Ground: _____ Mid Height: _____ Penthouse: _____ Elevator: Yes: _____ No: _____

View (Direction Facing): West: _____ East: _____ South: _____ North: _____

Obstructed View: Yes: _____ No: _____ Partial: _____ Details: _____

Parking: (Condominium): 1 parking: _____ 2 parking: _____ 3 parking: _____ Covered Parking: Yes: _____ No: _____

Monitored: Yes: _____ No: _____

Locker (Condominium): _____ Separate Locker: _____ In Unit: _____ Approximate Size: _____

Ensuite Laundry: Yes: _____ No: _____ Details: _____

Condominium Facilities: Pool: Yes: _____ No: _____ Gym/Fitness: Yes: _____ No: _____

Details: _____

Tennis/Racquet Ball: Yes: _____ No: _____ Meeting or Party Room: Yes: _____ No: _____

Security Guard: Yes: _____ No: _____ Details: _____

Concierge Services: Yes: _____ No: _____ Details: _____

Other Amenitities: _____

Pets Allowed: Yes: _____ No: _____ Details: _____

Marina: Yes: _____ No: _____ Boat Storage: Yes: _____ No: _____

Details: _____

Purchaser Approval Required: Yes: _____ No: _____ Details: _____

Condominium Fee Includes: _____

Special Assessments: _____

Other Condominium Info: _____

_____

Property Details

Exterior of Home: Brick: _____ Concrete: _____ Stone: _____ Stucco: _____ Aluminum Siding: _____

Wood: _____ Vinyl Siding: _____ Hardy-board: _____ Other: _____

Combination: _____

Foundation: Concrete: _____ Concrete Block: _____ Wood: _____ Other: _____

Roof: Shingles: _____ Tile: _____ Steel: _____ Shaker: _____ Other: _____

Age of Roof: _____ Details: _____

Bedrooms: Number of Bedrooms: _____

Bathrooms: Number of Bathrooms: _____ Full: _____ Partial: _____

Ensuite Bathroom: Yes: _____ No: _____ Separate Shower: _____ Separate Tub: _____

Comments: _____

Showers: Number of Showers: _____ Comments: _____

Closets: Walk-In: Yes: _____ No: _____ Organizers: _____

Details: _____

Basement: Finished: Yes: _____ No: _____ Walkout: _____ High Ceilings: _____ N/A: _____

Storage: _____ Workshop: _____

Elevator: _____

Heating: Gas: _____ Electric: _____ Oil: _____ Wood: _____ Age of Heating: _____

Air Conditioning: Central: _____ Window: _____ Age of A/C: _____

Electrical: _____

Water: _____

Sewage: _____

Garage: Attached: _____ Detached: _____

1 Car: _____ 2 Car: _____ 3 Car: _____ 4 Car: _____ Carport: _____ None: _____ Other: _____

Driveway: Private: _____ Shared: _____ Laneway: _____ None: _____ Other: _____

Kitchen Details: Eat-in: _____ Island: _____ Pantry: _____

Countertop Type: _____

Cabinetry: _____

Pantry: _____ Built-in Desk: _____ Double Sinks: _____

Built-in Shelves or Drawers: _____ Other: _____

Appliances: Fridge: _____ Stove: _____ Range: _____ Built-in Ovens: _____ Number of Ovens: _____

Convection: _____ Cooktop: _____ Gas: _____ Electric: _____ Propane: _____ Dishwasher: _____

Number of Dishwashers: _____ Microwave: _____ Warming Drawer: _____ Steamer: _____

Built-in Coffee Maker: _____ Ice Maker: _____ Cooler: _____ Freezer: _____ Water Filter: _____

Other: _____

Washer: _____ Dryer: _____ Details: _____

Outdoor Kitchen: Details: _____

Outdoor Patio: Concrete: _____ Pavers: _____ Wood: _____ Other: _____

Fireplace: _____ Lanai: _____ Screened Area: _____ Other: _____

Dining Room: Yes: _____ No: _____ Details: _____

Family Room/Great Room: Yes: _____ No: _____ Details: _____

Living Room: Yes: _____ No: _____ Details: _____

Office/Den: Yes: _____ No: _____ Location/Details: _____

Bonus Room: Yes: _____ No: _____ Details: _____

Theatre Room: Details: _____

Billiards Room: Details: _____

Other Rooms: Details: _____

Laundry Room: Main Level: _____ 2nd Floor: _____ Basement: _____ Other: _____

Flooring: Hardwood: _____ Parquet: _____ Carpet: _____ Tile: _____ Other: _____

Kitchen & Baths Flooring: Ceramic Tile: _____ Porcelain: _____ Natural Stone: _____ Vinyl: _____ Other: _____

Fireplace: Type(s): _____ Location(s): _____

Interior Features/Upgrades: _____

Window Coverings: _____

Decor/Paint Colour: _____

Internet and/or

Cable/Satellite: _____

Security System: Yes: _____ No: _____ Monitored: Yes: _____ No: _____ System Owned or Leased: _____

Number Control Pads: _____ Location: _____

Cameras: _____ Yes: _____ No: _____ Details: _____

Hot Water Tank: Owned: _____ Leased: _____ Tankless: _____ Details: _____

Swimming Pool: Yes: _____ No: _____ Heated: _____ Type of Heat: _____

Inground: _____ Yes: _____ No: _____ Gunite: _____ Vinyl: _____ Fibreglass: _____

Pool Cleaner: _____

Other: _____

Salt Water System: Yes: _____ No: _____

Hot Tub/Spa: Yes: _____ No: _____ Details: _____

Exterior Lighting: _____

Exterior Landscaping: _____

Other Upgrades or Features: _____

_____

_____

Overall Condition: _____

Area Amenities:

Recreation: _____

Golf: _____ Tennis: _____

Lake: _____ Inter-coastal: _____ Ocean: _____

Boat Launch: _____ Boat Dockage/Storage: _____

Water Skiing: _____ Fishing: _____

Beach: _____ Boardwalk: _____

Gym/Workout Facility: _____ Hiking/Jogging: _____

Country Club: _____

Dining: _____ Shopping: _____

Theatre: _____ Movies: _____

Museums: _____ Sport Facilities: _____

Music/Opera: _____ Art Gallery: _____

Park: _____ Church/Places of Worship: _____

Other: _____

_____

Hospital: _____ Doctor/Medical Facility: _____

Dentist: _____ Other Medical: _____

Police: _____ Fire Department: _____

Veterinary: _____ Other: _____

Overall Ranking: Excellent: _____ Good: _____ Satisfactory: _____ Poor: _____ Not Interested: _____

Additional Comments: _____

"I'm pleased for both of you and am confident that you will find something soon."

"We really like the one house we saw today. We're thinking about making an offer on it. But we'll see what Nina shows us tomorrow, compare them, and then decide. I'll keep you posted."

"Call me anytime. You are in good hands with Nina," reassured Terry.

"What has been especially helpful is the checklist you provided at one of the group meetings. Rob and I find it helps us keep track of the features of every house that we visit. We can't remember every detail of every property, so between the checklist and any photos we are given, we're able to compare details and ultimately weigh all our options," said Cathy.

"This is great to hear. Best of luck tomorrow."

Over dinner, Cathy and Rob reviewed the information sheet on the property they liked the best. Cathy was busy scribbling out numbers on a sheet of paper. "Rob, check this out," she said. "I realize that we are planning to buy a property for family use, but what do you think about renting out the house when we aren't using it? Take a look at this." She handed him the paper.

	No Income	Part-Time Income
Purchase price:	$300,000	$300,000
Mortgage (monthly payment): $200K @ 3.5 per cent: (approx)	$ 1,000	$ 1,000
Property tax/month:	$ 450	$ 450
Utilities/cable:	$ 600	$ 600
Property management fee:	$ 0	$ 450
Repairs and maintenance:	$ 100	$ 100
Insurance:	$ 110	$ 110

Total monthly costs:	$ 2,260	$ 2,710
Annual costs:	$27,120	$32,520
Weekly rental income (12 weeks):	$ 0	$ 1,500
Annual rental income:	$ 0	$ 18,000
Annual costs:	$ 27,120	$ 14,520
Difference:		$12,600

Rob reviewed the numbers. "Where did you come up with the rental income figures?"

Cathy replied, "I've been doing some research. I asked Nina to send me figures on what houses similar to what she planned to show us would rent for on a short-term basis, furnished. I also checked websites to get an idea of what other houses in the area were asking. From what I can see, the average weekly rental price in the area with similar square footage and value is approximately $1,500 to $1,700 per week—I went on the conservative side and used $1,500 in the calculation. It appears, depending on the website—and I assume the services offered—that the short-term management fees range from 30 to 50 per cent; so I used 30 per cent for these calculations—but it could be higher. We can't count on renting the property every week we aren't using it, but I figured we may be able to rent it the equivalent of one week a month, which equals about 12 weeks of rental."

"That's only about 20 per cent of the year. It seems very reasonable. I never really thought about it this way," said Rob.

"That's why you have me," kidded Cathy.

"How do you plan on finding part-time renters? Do you think we know enough people who would rent it for a total of 12 weeks?"

"I think we would be able to rent it ourselves for four to five weeks a year once we got the word out that it was available. For a family of four to rent an average hotel room, or possibly two hotel rooms, in the general area, it would cost between $150 and $300 per night.

For a three bedroom, three bath, double garage, and in-ground pool in a nice neighbourhood, $1,500 a week is a bargain.

"I've also been researching companies that manage short-term rentals for property owners. They advertise the availability of the property and ensure that the property is kept clean and secure for renters, for a fee that could be up to 30 to 50 per cent of the weekly rate. It sounds like a lot, but they take care of everything, including the maid service, and we may be able to rent the property more often. I thought we could enlist the service of one of these companies when we're not using the property. This could make up another five or six weeks—or maybe even more if we're lucky. Don't forget, any rental income is a bonus for us and helps to offset the annual costs," said Cathy.

"Makes sense to me," said Rob. He took another look at the figures. "We are not making any money, simply covering some of our costs. Over time this helps to pay off the mortgage. I hope, although I am not counting on it, that there will be appreciation in the future as well, not to mention the fact that it gives us a nice lifestyle. I like this."

Cathy responded, "I really like the house in the chain of lakes community that we viewed today. Nina mentioned that the sellers are very anxious, as they are relocating out of state. I think they begin their new jobs next week."

"I like the house as well. It's more than I thought we would get. If we don't see anything we like better tomorrow, I would be happy to make an offer on that house."

"I agree. Let's see what tomorrow brings."

* * *

Bright and early, Nina picked up Cathy and Rob. "We have another busy day ahead. I'm showing you two more houses in the community you like, along with several other houses in other neighbourhoods," she said.

"That's great. We both really like the house with the pool and spa in the chain of lakes community. Would it be possible to view this house again?" asked Cathy.

"Let me see if I can confirm an appointment for when we are in that community looking at a couple of other houses."

After spending the day viewing houses and neighbourhoods, and again walking through their choice property from the day before, Rob and Cathy concluded that the latter was their favourite.

"We really like this house—even more so after viewing it again," Cathy told Nina.

"Yes, I can see our family enjoying many happy years there," confirmed Rob.

"We have been contemplating making an offer on this house. Would it be possible for you to provide us with comparable sold-houses information for the area?" asked Cathy.

"Absolutely! I suggest that I drop you back at the hotel to relax and discuss this; in the meantime, I'll go to my office and prepare a contract for you to review, as well as assemble data of comparable sold houses," responded Nina.

Shortly after arriving back at the hotel, Cathy decided to call Terry. "We found a house, and we are making an offer!"

"That's great. Is it the one from yesterday that you described?"

"Yes. We went through it again today, along with about a dozen more houses, and we've decided it is the best one for us. Nina is completing an offer to purchase, as well as a list of comparable houses that have sold in the area. I just wanted to keep you updated on what's happening."

"Well, that's wonderful. I'm very excited for you," said Terry.

"The owners are relocating out of state—it's a job relocation, so they are motivated to sell. There isn't a lot for sale in this community—maybe four or five houses in total out of about 400 houses. I think this community is highly sought after. It's a gated community—with resort-like amenities, with its own downtown area, tennis facility, swimming pool, a gym, walking trails, and clubhouse. Also, the homeowners association takes care of all the exterior maintenance, including grass cutting, landscaping, and irrigation. We are so thrilled."

"Sounds fabulous. I am certain that Nina and the attorney will review everything with you and ensure the appropriate clauses and safeguards are in place."

"Thank you, Terry, for your vote of confidence. I am just so excited and wanted to share this with you," said Cathy.

"I'm happy for you and Rob. Good luck with your offer," Terry said before hanging up.

Forty-five minutes later, Nina called to say she was on her way back to the hotel and asked if they would meet her in the coffee shop.

"Let's begin reviewing the sales data in the neighbourhood and general area," Nina recommended. "As you can see, there has not been a great deal of activity in this community. During the last nine months, there have been six sales, all of which have sold within 60 days of being listed and for 95 per cent or more of the listing price. The list price of the subject property is within the sales price range of comparably sized and appointed houses in the community. This is a very-high-demand community, partly because of the schools in the area but also because of the amenities and proximity to transportation. These are very good stats, especially given the economic situation."

"Here are the comparable sold stats in the general area, excluding the community you are considering." Nina handed Cathy and Rob a sheaf of papers. "Although the sold data in the general area is satisfactory, the properties have averaged four months on the market, and pricing is not as tight. And there is more for sale."

"What a difference. Why is this?" asked Rob.

"There are five highly rated schools that service the community you are considering, whereas only a couple of them serve the adjacent communities. In addition, the amenities in the community, along with the many lake and canal views, are attractive. There hasn't been the same numbers of foreclosures in this community; therefore, it hasn't experienced a decline in pricing as in other neighbourhoods. This is a highly sought-after community."

"Shouldn't that be good for long-term resale once the economy and real estate market recover?" asked Rob.

"Normally, this is the case," replied Nina. "The sellers are serious, as they are being relocated by their employer. It is likely that the transferring company understands the economy as well as the importance of a smooth transition to another state; you may have an advantage here."

"Given the location, do you think this would be a desirable property to rent on a short-term basis?" asked Cathy.

"Well, you'd be located very close to many amenities that snowbird renters frequent, and ease of access to the property is ideal. You should check with the homeowners association to confirm that it allows short-term rentals. I think the HOA will require a minimum of six months' rental in this community to ensure stability."

"I didn't realize that there could be restrictions; I guess we'll need to find this out before we rent the property. Fortunately, we are not counting on rental income in order to purchase the property—it was just a thought," said Cathy.

"It is important that you understand all of the rules of the homeowners association. I'll try to get the documentation from the association that outlines the rules and regulations."

"I'm aware there is an annual homeowners association fee and that the HOA maintains the exterior and common grounds. I'm looking forward to learning more about the association," Cathy said.

After reviewing and discussing the stats, it was agreed that Rob and Cathy would offer $285,000 (the house was listed for $325,000) with a 30-day closing date and an escrow deposit of $10,000 to show good faith. The offer included conditions for property, pool, and termite (and other pest) inspections. There was no finance condition, as it was a cash offer; their financing was already arranged and approved in Canada.

If financing is required and not as yet finalized, speak with the real estate professional or your lawyer about including a condition on arranging a mortgage. Ask the real estate broker to explain the disclosure and other state-specific rules. If it is a financed deal, it's a good strategy to provide a preapproval letter with the offer, as it adds strength to the deal.

Nina suggested that the offer of a cash purchase without a finance condition added strength to the offer to purchase. The house was in immaculate condition, and she didn't expect the inspections to turn up any major problems; the inspections are a due diligence.

Nina stated that she would request a copy of the seller disclosure form that the seller fills out, which provides information about the home, as she reviewed the preprinted clauses, addendum, and disclosure paperwork.

Disclosures and other documentation may vary by state.

Cathy advised Nina, "The offer to purchase should be in the name of the trust."

"Ah, that was my next question. What name do you intend to put on the contract?" asked Nina.

"Our cross-border attorney created a trust for us and instructed us to make the offer to purchase in the name of the trust, as this is how it will be titled," said Rob.

"Should a lawyer read the offer to purchase, review the title, or be involved at this stage?" asked Cathy.

"If you would like to have an attorney review the contract and be part of the closing process, we can definitely arrange for that. In Florida, transactions are either managed and closed by title companies or by attorneys. Do you have a specific attorney in mind?" asked Nina.

Cathy responded, "In Ontario, a real estate lawyer completes the closing; we are not sure how the process works in Florida. We don't know of any lawyers here. Our lawyer in Ontario who set up our trust offered to review the contract. Or perhaps you can point us in the right direction?"

"I can suggest a few local real estate attorneys whom previous clients have been happy with, if you like; or consider asking your attorney if he or she could recommend a local contact here," offered Nina.

Cathy said, "Good idea—I'll contact my lawyer in Ontario to find out what he suggests. In the meantime, I will fax the contract to him."

Once all the paperwork was signed, Nina said she would contact Lindy, the seller's agent, and then would begin the process.

Later that evening, Nina returned to Cathy and Rob with a counteroffer. She explained, "Lindy was able to reach the sellers, who are out of town, and we had a conference call. I found out that the sellers are able to negotiate the offer without needing the approval from their employer. The sellers have agreed to the closing date and all the conditions in the offer; they have also agreed to provide the seller property disclosure. In addition, they have a copy of the survey and all warranties for the property. The only thing they changed was the price," explained Nina, telling them the sellers' counteroffer.

"That's approximately $10,000 off their list price. Did they include all the appliances and window coverings?" asked Rob.

"Yes, everything is included, with no other changes," replied Nina.

"Rob and I really do not want to go that high. Do you think they will come down any more?" asked Cathy.

"Well, one way to find out is to try. Despite that this is a highly desirable community, at this time there are no other contracts on the table," said Nina.

"Why don't we change the contract price and see what happens?" suggested Rob.

Cathy nodded in agreement. "Okay, let's try $292,000. Also, I spoke with our lawyer in Toronto, who connected me with an attorney in Florida who has read the offer to purchase; he said everything in the offer looked fine."

"Terrific!" Nina said. "Do you want to have this local attorney participate in closing the transaction as well?"

"Yes, assuming we make a deal," Rob said.

Once all the changes were made and initialed, Nina set out to present the counteroffer, telling them that she would be in touch. A few hours later, Nina called to advise she was heading back and that the seller did not accept their offer but instead recountered.

When Nina returned, Cathy asked, "Can you give us a rough idea of approximately what our closing costs and obligations will be? This will help us determine how we wish to proceed."

Nine responded, "In the state of Florida, you will be presented with a two-page closing statement called a HUD-1 Settlement Statement, which itemizes the financial obligations of both the seller and buyer. It sets forth the net proceeds amount due to the seller and the amount of funds needed to close from the buyer.

"There are two types of documentary stamps, or doc stamps as we call them. One is for the deed or transfer of title, and the other is for registration of a mortgage. In this county, often the seller pays the documentary stamps on the deed. The buyer pays the doc stamps and what is known as intangible tax if a mortgage is registered. As your mortgage is in Canada and not collateralized against the U.S. property, you will not be recording a mortgage in Florida and therefore will not be paying doc stamps or intangible tax on a mortgage."

"What you call doc stamps must be similar to the land transfer tax that we pay in Canada," commented Cathy.

"The formula to determine the amount is to multiply the purchase price by $0.70 per $100 (or any portion thereof) for the transfer of real property—known as documentary stamps," Nina explained. "As for the mortgage doc stamps, the rate is $0.35 per $100 (or any portion thereof) for a new mortgage. The seller is paying the doc stamps," advised Nina.

Exception: in Miami-Dade County FL, the rate is $0.60 per $100 (or any portion thereof) plus $0.45 per $100 surtax on documents that transfer anything other than a single family residence.

Rates vary depending on state and/or county. Ask your real estate agent or attorney to advise of the specific details relevant to the state you are purchasing in.

"Since our mortgage is in Canada, we won't be required to pay doc stamps or intangible tax on the mortgage, as it is not registered here?" asked Rob.

"That is correct," replied Nina. "The property tax and homeowners association annual amounts for the property will be prorated. In this county, property tax invoices are mailed in the fall; they're due in April of the following year. Should you decide to pay your property taxes early, you will be given a discount on the amount due—something for you to keep in mind for the future.

"However, the title company or attorney closing the deal will determine if the property taxes and HOA fees—the homeowners association fees—have been paid in full and prorate the amount relative to the closing date. This will be shown as an adjustment on the HUD-1 settlement statement. Other costs may include a title policy, of which there is normally an owner's policy as well as a separate mortgage policy (if there is a mortgage on the property), title company and/or legal fees, and recording costs.

"On the seller's side of the HUD-1 settlement statement, there will be real estate fees, documentary stamps for the deed, the title insurance policy, and other incidentals," said Nina.

"I'm glad the sellers pay for the title policy and deed doc stamps—$300,000 × $0.70/$100 is about $2,100!" said Cathy.

For example purposes—if there was a U.S. mortgage of $200,000 registered in this county and state, the doc stamps on the mortgage would equal $700 ($200,000 × $0.35 per $100 (or portion thereof)), and the intangible tax on the mortgage would equal $400 ($200,000 × $0.20 per $100 (or portion thereof)). Consult with a real estate professional or your attorney for details on documentary stamps (which a Canadian may know as a land transfer tax) for the deed, as well as documentary stamps and intangible tax on the mortgage. Taxes and stamps will vary depending on the state and county.

Nina suggested, "Ask your attorney to quote their fee. The title company or attorney will send a copy of the HUD-1 prior to closing for your review, approval, and signature."

"And with respect to your fee, just to reconfirm, you said when we first spoke that you are paid by the real estate company or something to that effect," said Rob.

"When the sellers listed their property for sale, they agreed to pay a fee or commission to their agent, the listing company. A portion of that fee is payable to another brokerage should that brokerage procure an accepted offer. The real estate fees come off the top of the purchase price on the completion date and are distributed on closing by the title company or attorney to the real estate brokerages," said Nina.

"This is how we have done it back home," said Cathy.

"The other costs that you will likely incur are a property inspection fee, which is typically in the $500 to $1000 range for this type of house; the pool inspection—approximately $150; and termite and other pest inspection fees in the $300 to $500 range—there is a termite and pest inspection condition in your offer. There also may be a fee to obtain an estoppel certificate from your HOA, which is typically in the $100 to $200 range, and you will need to arrange property insurance, the cost of which will vary depending on the insurer, your deductible, and the type of policy and coverage you require. It is important that you obtain property insurance quotes and arrange property insurance, including liability insurance, as soon as possible after you have an accepted offer," said Nina.

"Has the lender advised you about points and how they charge for their services?" she then asked.

"We were told about points and fees if we were arranging a mortgage in the U.S. Our mortgage is from our Canadian bank and is already set up. We've already paid for the appraisal, registration, and legal expense. Everything is finalized, and we have no other fees or expenses with respect to our mortgage," Cathy told her.

"Friends of ours who paid cash for a brand-new property with no mortgage told us in passing that they were charged for things they weren't expecting," Cathy continued.

"With new-house purchases from a builder—or any real estate purchase, for that matter—the buyer should pay special attention to the contract where it outlines who is responsible for what closing costs. Some builders have most of the closing costs on the buyer's side of the HUD in a cash sale, and the contract may have the builder choose the title company. It's a good idea to have a local real estate attorney review all of the documents, survey, and title policy; sometimes the title company is owned by or affiliated to the builder."

"That's interesting. We feel comfortable, as our lawyer has reviewed the agreement. Given our budget, the comparable sold information, and how we feel about the property, we would like to proceed with a counteroffer," said Cathy.

Nina made the requested changes to the contract.

"Please tell them this is our final offer," Rob said.

"I'll make sure they know exactly your position," said Nina. "I'll be back in touch soon."

"Good luck," said Cathy.

After Nina departed, Rob and Cathy decided to drive to the outlet mall. Cathy had remembered how great the sales were there on a previous vacation and thought it would be a good distraction—she wanted to think about something other than the negotiations.

"Did you really mean this was our final offer?" asked Cathy.

Rob laughed. "Well, yes and no. You can make the final decision."

Cathy rolled her eyes and smiled back. "Let's see what happens."

Much to Cathy and Rob's surprise, the outlet mall had a big sale going on, with markdowns between 50 and 70 per cent. After finding some great bargains they stopped to have iced tea. "This seems to be taking a long time. I wonder what is happening?" Cathy asked. Then the phone rang.

"Well, congratulations, your offer has been accepted," Nina said.

Cathy almost dropped the phone. "Yes! They accepted! Thank you, Nina. We were wondering what was taking so long. This is great news. Now what do we need to do?" asked Cathy.

"I'll meet you to give you your copy of the contract, at which time I will also review the next steps. Shall we meet in the hotel restaurant, say in 35 minutes?' asked Nina.

"Great! We will see you there."

Cathy gave Rob a big grin. "We did it! We're meeting Nina at the hotel restaurant in 35 minutes to finish up the paperwork and get the details on our next steps."

On the drive back to the hotel, Cathy said, "I want to call Terry. Should I? Do you think she will think I'm bothering her?"

"Go for it. She will be thrilled," said Rob.

So Cathy called Terry. "We got a deal—they accepted," Cathy blurted out just as Terry answered "hello."

"Great! Congratulations. I am happy for you two," said Terry. Cathy enthusiastically gave Terry the details of their house.

At the restaurant, Nina completed and distributed the final paperwork. She gave Cathy and Rob a list of several property, pool, and termite inspectors and suggested they book the inspections as soon as possible.

Cathy said, "We are not scheduled to fly back to Toronto for two days; do you recommend that we try to book the inspections while we are here so that we can attend?"

Nina replied, "If you can book the inspections while you are in town, that would be ideal. I think you should attend the inspections and review all the items in the house with the various inspectors while you're here. Once you have the inspectors booked, let me know so that I can advise the sellers.

"Lastly, I will need to deliver the escrow deposit to the title company to hold in trust, pending completion. I'll look after this tomorrow morning. Would you like me to fax the contract and documents to your Florida attorney as well?" asked Nina.

"Yes, that would be great. I'll give you his contact information and I'll also contact him to let him know we have a deal," replied Cathy.

"While we are completing the inspections, just a reminder that you should also obtain property insurance quotes and commitments:

you want to ensure that the property has appropriate insurance coverage for closing," said Nina.

The next morning Cathy was up early to book the house, pool, and termite inspections. By mid-morning she informed Nina that the home, pool, and termite inspectors were confirmed for the following day, all at 9 a.m. Rob and Cathy decided they wanted to attend the inspections, as they wanted to learn more about their house. Cathy also informed Nina that the attorney received the paperwork and that she had made property insurance arrangements—everything was falling into place.

For the rest of the day, Rob and Cathy decided to enjoy Florida and all it had to offer, including the sunny, warm climate that they would get to enjoy for many winters to come.

The next morning they met the inspectors and Nina at the property. Cathy had her fingers crossed that all the inspections would be fine. Now that they had come this far, she did not want any problems.

Rick, the house inspector, as well as the termite/pest and pool inspectors, were thorough. Cathy and Rob spent several hours going through the house in great detail with Rick, watching him visually check all accessible systems and components of the house, including the electrical, plumbing, heating, and cooling, as well as ensure that the structural components such as the foundation, roof, and windows were to code and in good repair. Rick also checked the insulation and irrigation systems, and all chattels and fixtures to ensure they were operating properly. Rick reported that the house was in good condition, needing only routine minor maintenance, and presented Rob and Cathy with a written report and a maintenance checklist. Tom, the pool inspector, also gave the pool and pool equipment a good report.

Gerry, the termite inspector, explained that his firm was licensed with the USDA and a member of the state association; he gave Cathy and Rob a brochure outlining his qualifications. His report confirmed that there was no evidence of subterranean termites or carpenter ants. Gerry suggested that they consider obtaining a termite bond that was renewable each year, which gives some protection should their house attract termites. He also suggested that they have the house inspected annually for termites as part of their routine annual maintenance—annual termite inspection is common in Florida.

Rob and Cathy were thrilled by the results of the inspections. Later that afternoon they were off to the airport for their return flight to Toronto. They told Nina that they would be in touch once they heard back from the lender.

Cathy also spoke with an insurance broker to get quotes from several insurance companies and arrange house and liability coverage. The insurance broker asked several questions about the size and age of the house, the number of bedrooms and bathrooms, garage, heating and air conditioning systems, type of roof, swimming pool, and other house-related features. Cathy explained to the insurance broker that it was a vacation property and that they would be there part time, as their permanent residence was in Canada. This is an important item to disclose to an insurance company, as it could be a factor in the type of policy you obtain. She and the broker discussed third-party liability coverage amounts and reviewed deductible options, as well as hurricane and flood coverage. Cathy explained that the property would be titled to an irrevocable trust, something the insurance broker was familiar with. The insurance broker reviewed the details of the insurance policy, as well as any exclusions, and assured Cathy that the policy would be sent to her that week.

Cathy then contacted Nina and asked if she and Rob needed to attend the closing in Florida and if so, when would this occur?

Nina replied, "You are certainly welcome to attend the closing, which is set for next Friday—but it's not necessary. Your attorney can send the documents by courier for signature and notarization."

The next day, Cathy spoke with the attorney, who confirmed that the closing would be moved up by a week to the coming Friday. Cathy informed the attorney that she and Rob would not be attending the closing in Florida and requested that the documents be couriered for signature.

A few days later, Cathy received the couriered documents for review and signature. She and Rob met with a notary public in Toronto, as Florida law mandates that some of the documents be signed and notarized. Documents that required signature included:

- HUD-1 settlement statement
- Escrow disbursement agreement
- Compliance agreement
- Survey affidavit
- Name affidavit
- Mortgage documents*
- Good faith estimate*
- Truth in lending document*
- Interest statement*

The signed and notarized documents were sent by overnight courier to the attorney, and arrangements for wire transfer of funds for the closing was arranged. The following week, Cathy and Rob were thrilled that the trust owned the property.

This is one example of closing costs and process. Understand that processes, closing costs, and who pays for what may vary from transaction to transaction, as well as depend on the state and county. Closing fees and expenses may also vary depending on whether you are purchasing a new property from a builder or a resale property. Be sure to read the fine print. Ask for a breakdown of all costs in advance. It is prudent to consult with a legal professional for advice.

---

*Applicable if there is a mortgage.

CHAPTER 13

How to Buy Distressed Real Estate

Over the course of the next few weeks, several of the parents who had participated in the meetings were busy gathering information, arranging appointments, and meeting with mortgage and cross-border professionals to discuss their individual needs and situation. Michelle and David, as well as J.P. and Mary, were now in the process of researching types of properties they could purchase based on their preapproved lending criteria. Terry introduced them to real estate brokers in their chosen cities to help both couples find desirable properties, conduct due diligence, and ultimately make an offer to purchase.

As Terry explained to them, not all real estate professionals are the same; while they may have the same type of license, their level of experience and areas of specialization may differ. Real estate professionals perform different real estate services—the most common is to find and show properties within the buyer's budget that match the buyer's geographic preferences and suit his or her wants and needs as determined by the Property Profile. The real estate professional can also assist in providing general pricing and sales trends in the area, as well as inform the buyer about amenities and other local information. The real estate broker can also complete and present the purchase and sale agreement to the seller's broker.

While doing her research, Mary wanted clarification about aspects of distressed real estate, so she called Terry. "Can you tell me what is meant by a short sale and foreclosure? Kate, the real estate broker, has sent me a package of properties to review. Some have notations in the copy about being a short sale or foreclosure. How does this work?"

Terry replied, "That's an aspect of buying a property in the U.S. that I've been thinking about introducing to the group. The process is a little more complex than a straightforward sale. Here's what I suggest. Let me find out if there is interest with the group to hold another meeting. Coincidentally, I received e-mails today from others in the group with the same question. I think that you, as well as other Canadian buyers, will come across this during the search process; it's a good topic to review in depth."

"That would be fantastic. I've heard about the U.S. real estate market and people losing their homes, but I don't know what this means. Let me know if you set up a meeting and when," said Mary.

Terry replied, "I'll send a group e-mail with a proposal to meet this coming Saturday morning. I will be in touch."

The group responded positively to the meeting invitation. Cathy assisted Terry in booking the room at the arena and arranging for coffee and muffins.

Terry welcomed the parents to the meeting, then said, "I would like to introduce two surprise guests who have agreed to join our meeting. Patricia is a U.S. real estate broker who will spend some time addressing foreclosures and other types of real estate sales, and Monique will be reviewing the importance of private health care insurance. These are two topics that I have received several questions about, so I thought it would be helpful to cover them."

"Fabulous—Roger and I were wondering how this process of foreclosures and bank sales worked, and how we go about finding them," said Helen.

"I agree. I have heard about getting a deal on a bank-foreclosed home, but I have also heard that sometimes these properties are in very poor condition. It makes me wonder if it is really worth it. And out-of-province health insurance is so important. I work in a hospital and have heard unfortunate stories about accident and illness while out of province and the costs involved," commented Michelle.

Terry motioned for Patricia to take over the meeting. "I have known Patricia for over 25 years; after college we chose the same career path, just in different locations. Patricia lives in Florida, but she is in town this week attending a wedding as well as her son's university graduation. She called me last night to see if we could meet for lunch and has graciously agreed to join the group today."

Patricia smiled. "Hello, I am delighted to be here to share information on a topic near and dear to me—real estate. I will review foreclosures and short sales, as well as the pros and cons and process of buying these types of properties," replied Patricia as she proceeded to hand out a small booklet.

She continued, "When homeowners, or borrowers, fall behind in making their payments to the lender—in other words, default on making their required mortgage payments—the lender, usually after a period of time, attempts to contact the borrowers to work out an arrangement. Each state has its own rules and timeframes about how the foreclosure process is handled. Ultimately, the goal of the lender is to collect the outstanding mortgage monies due, even if this results in having to auction the property.

"The recent downturn in the housing market, combined with the potential discount possible with a foreclosed property, could mean a bigger potential payoff in the future. Despite initiatives to contain the rising tide of foreclosures, the number of default notices, sales notices, and foreclosure and short sales these last few years is higher than I have ever seen. Millions of U.S. properties have gone into foreclosure. This presents you with an opportunity to purchase property at a reduced price. Foreclosed properties may be purchased, depending on the location and inventory, for a discount on their potential market value."

The Foreclosure Process

Patricia paused for a moment and then continued, "Many people ask me about purchasing a foreclosed property—and, yes, there are opportunities to acquire a property under value. But there may also be risks and, in some cases, the process can take several months. These properties may require work; you will need to estimate the cost to bring the property to the standards you are accustomed to and then determine whether the purchase price is appropriate.

"There are experienced buyers—investors—who treat buying foreclosed and other distressed property as a business—that is, they research and acquire these properties, both at the pre-foreclosure as well as the foreclosure auction stage. These buyers purchase the properties and perhaps invest some money in basic renovations and then remarket the properties. This is known as the buy-fix-flip strategy. These experienced buyers understand the process, they know their way around the courthouse, and they often have contacts in the loss mitigation departments of the various lenders. When buying a pre-foreclosure or foreclosure auction property, the buyer normally acquires the property 'as is,' which may include liens and possibly even occupants. The outstanding balance of the mortgage may be more than the value of the property. Of course, these buyers don't usually pay more than the projected market value; they negotiate with the loss mitigation department of the lender and agree upon a price that is acceptable to both parties.

"Before agreeing on a purchase, it is important that a buyer does his or her homework—such as hiring a contractor to complete a home inspection to check the structure and operating systems. A title company or an attorney should complete a title search to determine if there are any outstanding liens or clouds on title—that is, some kind of defect on title—or open permits. A real estate professional or appraiser can provide a comparable market analysis, which helps to determine the value of comparable real estate in the area.

"All of this takes time—sometimes many months. These properties can be in a poor state of repair. After acquisition, sometimes the buyer may need to clean up and repair the property. Careful planning and consultation with appropriate professionals is recommended to properly determine the cost and time it will take to bring the property to good condition; this all needs to be factored into the budget and purchase price."

Patricia paused briefly, then went on. "Obviously these buyers are taking on risk and will only do so if and when they can acquire the property at a discount on market value. Once the property has been purchased, any liens are extinguished, occupants are moved, and the property is cleaned up and repaired. The buyer may offer the property for sale to the open market at an attractive price, which includes a premium for his or her time and costs.

"Something important to understand is that if a buyer intends to flip or lease the property, he or she may have to disclose that the property is not being bought for personal use. At closing, the seller— the lender—may require the buyer to sign an affidavit; in other words, the buyer cannot say that the property is for personal use and then flip it. Keep in mind that some foreclosure properties listed for sale with a real estate brokerage have what is referred to as a 'first look,' for primary buyers only.

"Buying foreclosed auction properties is not likely the route a Canadian buyer would go, as it takes a lot of time and you really need to be knowledgeable about how to navigate through the courthouse and the lender's loss mitigation department. Many experienced investors have contacts within lenders' departments, and these contacts help to facilitate the process. Keep in mind that you would be competing with experienced buyers who reside in the city who do this as a business. That said, real estate professionals can be a great source of foreclosed and short sales properties. It is also important that you ask if there are any rules about purchasing the foreclosed property.

"Please take a look at the second page of the booklet I handed out; let's review the descriptions of different foreclosure stages," said Patricia.

Stages:

1. **Default and pre-foreclosure**—When a borrower has defaulted on the required mortgage loan payment, normally after a period of time (and after several attempts to rectify the situation), the lender begins the foreclosure process. The goal of the lender is to retrieve the money lent.

   Depending on the state, the lender may solicit the services of a trustee to facilitate the foreclosure. Duties of the trustee include advertising the property for a required timeframe before the auction (timeframes vary based on the state). For example, in the state of Florida, the lender usually issues a notice of default, which is recorded in the circuit court, making it public knowledge that the property is in default. This is known as the pre-foreclosure period. During this time, the borrower/owner of the property may be able to remedy the default by refinancing or working out a payment plan with the lender.

   While the property is in pre-foreclosure, the borrower may offer the property for sale, and a buyer can offer to purchase the home. If the owner receives an offer to purchase the home for less than the value of the mortgage, the owner can ask the lender if it will agree to a short sale, also referred to as a "short payoff" (discussed below).

2. **Foreclosure auction**—After a period of time (the timeframe varies by state), a notice of sale is issued, setting a foreclosure auction date. The notice must be advertised for a period of time (which again varies by state). By the auction date, if the default is not remedied, the property may be put up for sale at the auction. The opening bid may be the outstanding loan plus costs, or some auctions start at a discounted price—it varies depending on the lender, the type of loan, and other factors. Anyone can bid at the auction, with the property going to the highest bidder; it usually must be paid for in full at the auction itself. The buyer receives the property in "as is" condition, which may include existing liens and possibly even occupants.

It is important that the buyer knows the market value of the property before the auction, as the foreclosed property may have no equity, or even negative equity versus the opening bid. If nobody bids higher than the opening bid, the property goes back to the lender and becomes a lender-owned property, also known as real estate owned, or REO. At this point the lender usually does minor clean up and repair, may remove any liens, and if necessary arranges to have any tenants or occupants vacate, then lists the property for sale with a real estate professional. Some buyers have been able to purchase REOs directly from the lender before the lender lists it for sale.

3. **Short sale**—An owner in the pre-foreclosure stage may offer the property for sale before the auction. If, after reviewing the sales of comparable homes in the area, it is determined that the value of the property is less than the outstanding mortgage balance, the owner might attempt to negotiate with the lender to accept a short sale, which is an amount less than the outstanding mortgage balance. The owner is motivated to try to sell the property before the foreclosure auction. You want to make sure that that there are no other liens on the property. Ultimately, the lender has the control and authority to approve or deny any offer to purchase for less than the outstanding debt (unless the seller is willing and able to pay the difference between the sales price and mortgage amount and costs). It can take a long time to get an answer from the lender on short sales, and some offers do not get approved by the lender.

4. **REO (real estate owned)**—Once a property has gone through the pre-foreclosure and auction stages (outlined above) and if it was not purchased at the auction, perhaps due to the outstanding loan balance plus costs (which may be the opening bid at the auction) being more than the value of the property, the property is owned by the lender. Banks and lenders are generally not in the business of home renovation and may have an inventory of residential properties in poor repair. These properties will be priced taking into consideration the value of similar properties in the area, and the condition of the

property, among other things. An REO purchased property may be a quicker purchase process than a short sale purchase and is often sold vacant. The lender may include an addendum to the purchase contract, which should be read carefully, as there may be "exceptions." It is important to review the terms and conditions contained in the addendum, since it forms part of the agreement and may, in the event of a conflict, supersede any previously agreed to terms and conditions in the purchase and sale contract. It is important to consult a real estate attorney for advice prior to signing the agreement.

"My gosh, I didn't realize this was such as process," said David.

"Patricia, to confirm that I understand the pre-foreclosure process, there are potential deals in buying a property in foreclosure. However, to get those deals at a discount, I may need to do research at the courthouse, negotiate with the lender if the outstanding debt is more than the value of the home—which means I would need to have access to the home and have it appraised—then work with a lawyer to remove any possible liens and possibly to handle vacating occupants, and then probably having to repair the property. Is that right?" asked Marty.

"Pre-foreclosure is the stage before the foreclosure auction occurs," replied Patricia. "Alternatively, you could be a bidder at the foreclosure auction—you really should be aware of the condition of the property, the cost to refurbish where applicable, if there are other liens, as well as the market value of the property before the foreclosure auction sale."

"Got it. This is not realistic for me to do—and I haven't any clue of what I am doing. I think I will leave this for the others and pay a little more—the wholesale price," said Lindsey.

Patricia replied, "Some buyers wait for the lender to acquire the property and then offer the property for sale (as an REO). But I think it is important to understand the pre-foreclosure and foreclosure auction process so that you understand the differences between foreclosure auction purchases, short sales, and REOs."

REO Purchase

Patricia continued, "'REO' stands for 'real estate owned' in Florida. If a buyer does not purchase the property at the foreclosure auction, the lender forecloses. With a foreclosure auction sale, the buyer assumes the risk and may be required to pay cash for the property on the day of the auction. This is not the case with an REO property. Some lenders may offer to finance the property to qualified buyers.

"Keep in mind that the lender is motivated to the sell the property, as it isn't in the business of holding real estate for nonperforming loans. At the same time, the lender wants to get as much money as possible for the home, since it is potentially taking a loss against the original mortgage. It is important that you obtain an appraisal or professional opinion of value of the property to ensure that you confirm the purchase price is in line with the value of the property. The real estate professional will be able to provide you with comparative sales data in the area. In addition, you will likely view other properties in the neighbourhood to get a sense of the value. Be wary of being attracted to areas with high foreclosure rates and high inventories based on price alone. Consider all the information related to price and property condition, as well as sales trends.

"If the property requires renovation, it is also prudent to obtain quotes from contractors. Common economical ways that homes can be refurbished include painting, installing new flooring—such as tile, carpet, or even hardwood—updating cabinetry and countertops in the kitchen and possibly the bathrooms, and updating the appliances. Costlier renovations may include windows, roof, plumbing, electrical, and heating and air conditioning systems. Consider having a professional property inspection of the property and operating systems; you don't want any unpleasant surprises. Evaluate the property from both the point of view of financial distress as well as physical distress. Bargains do exist—do your homework; you don't want to end up with major renovation headaches that you didn't factor into the plan."

"Do REO properties come with liens and occupants, and are they in poor condition?" asked Laura.

"The good news is often they do not come with liens or occupants; usually the lender deals with this. The condition varies; some are quite clean, others are poor, and then there's everything in between. It is a good idea to view any property that you contemplate purchasing to see the condition before submitting an offer to purchase. It is tough to buy a property after just viewing photos over the Internet. This is an investment; consider spending the time to go to the city and view a selection of properties," responded Patricia.

David commented, "Buying distressed property involves a great deal of research and work; there is a lot to consider. I can understand why having a plan is important."

"Yes, having a well-thought-out plan, financial budget, and systems in place is important," said Patricia. "It can be difficult for inexperienced investors to begin with a buy-fix-flip strategy as their first investment plan. Although some foreclosure and short sale properties may represent good value relative to the market value, it is important to be aware of the costs and time involved in refurbishing a property and budget accordingly. If you find a distressed property that you wish to pursue as an investment property, perhaps consider a buy-hold strategy; this gives you time to better understand the market and establish contacts with renovators or contractors. As an investor, it's very important to have information about rental income as well as vacancy rates—and be realistic. Be aware of inflated values that may suggest you might get a higher rent than what is reality. Have a lot of comparable local data. Consult with a local real estate professional or property manager."

Marty said, "It's also important to understand other costs in addition to repairs, such as annual property tax, insurance, HOA or condo monthly fees, utilities, and mortgage payments, to compare with the likely rental income in order to figure out if the property is worth pursuing."

"And remember to factor in property management fees if you are working with a professional, as well as accounting and legal fees, and a vacancy allowance. In addition, understand your exit strategy before you begin," noted Patricia.

"Patricia, do most Canadians buy a property on their first visit to the state they've chosen to purchase in, or does the buying process entail a number of visits?" asked Eliza.

"Great question. The answer is, it depends. I have known buyers to spend a week in the state and acquire a property. Understand that you will likely have had in-depth conversations with your U.S. real estate professional about your needs, wants, goals, and budget before visiting the city. Your financing, where applicable, has been arranged ahead of time; you are simply waiting for the right property. The real estate professional may send you an information package educating you on neighbourhoods, house styles, amenities, pricing, and trends and including examples of properties fitting your needs, wants, and budget. Before your visit, the real estate professional will usually continue to update you on appropriate properties as they become available.

"During your visit, the real estate professional will try to make the most of your time; he or she will have set up visits to properties and neighbourhoods based on your discussions. In some cities there are a number of properties on the market at any given time; therefore, it is possible that you may accomplish your mission on your first trip. Should you not find the suitable property on your first trip, you will probably be successful within one or two more visits. Based on your feedback from the first trip, the real estate professional can keep you updated on any newly listed properties and can be prepared to act quickly once a suitable property is available," said Patricia.

"It is sort of like relocating; when David's company moved us from the west coast we visited southern Ontario for a week and bought a home. We were very educated before making that trip despite that we had never previously visited the city. You are right—the real estate broker was excellent and did assist us greatly in our mission to find a home. This sounds like a similar process," said Michelle.

Patricia replied, "It is similar but also somewhat different. Although you want to be in a good neighbourhood with good schools and amenities, your focus is a little different, as you aren't worried about registering children for schools and where the children's recreational facilities are and so on. Your focus is more on your leisure activities."

"Yes, like where is the nearest golf and tennis facilities," said Rob with a chuckle.

Short Sale Purchase

"Let's finish with short sale properties," Terry said, smiling at Patricia.

"A short sale property is a sale that the lender is willing to allow to occur, as it has agreed to take less than the outstanding mortgage debt," Patricia continued. "With the decline in property values these last few years, lenders have found themselves in a position of having a number of loans in default—so many properties, in fact, that they may not have enough staff to manage these properties. Meanwhile, these properties need maintenance—grass, perhaps pool maintenance, utilities, insurance, HOA fees, and so on. All this costs the lender time and money, and yet it is not receiving any income from the property or the nonperforming loan.

"Many owners, knowing that they will eventually lose their home to a foreclosure auction, may not pay the city property tax or HOA or condo fees. These items rank first in priority over the lender's mortgage loan, therefore, if the lender acquires the property, it is the lender that will be required to bring these items current," advised Patricia.

She continued, "For these reasons and to get a nonperforming loan off the books, sometimes a lender is willing to allow a short sale. The owner may list the home for sale with a real estate broker and, in advance, the owner or the real estate professional or lawyer can try to negotiate a sale price that would be acceptable to the lender. The process to get a short sale approved may take three or four months, possibly longer, and some short sales don't get approved. There are such things as approved short sales whereby the price is set by the lender; the timeframe to closing for one of these is usually shorter. You may also come across an approved short sale after a cancellation by a buyer—the buyer may have made an offer that the bank counter-offered. If the buyer walks, the agent for the seller will remarket the home at the approved price. Your real estate professional will explain the process and types of properties available that are being sold as short sales."

"I guess you are confirming what I had thought—that there are bargains out there. It just takes some time, patience, and digging to find them," said J.P.

"There certainly are opportunities; property values have declined these last few years, and with the low-interest-rate environment, coupled with our strong Canadian dollar, this has certainly been an opportune time for Canadian buyers," replied Patricia.

"That's why we're here!" said Michelle.

Patricia continued: "I have described the foreclosure process based on my experience in Florida. Keep in mind that other states may have different processes, timeframes, and laws for distressed sales and/or mortgage loans that are in default. For example, some states have a power of sale process—it is important that you work with an experienced local real estate professional and attorney who can explain the processes and rules."

"The real estate brokers that Terry introduced us to in Arizona have been very helpful; the processes and real estate market have been explained to us in depth," said David.

"Thank you, Patricia. I am sure that this information provides a great deal of food for thought for anyone considering foreclosed or other distressed property. Now, why don't we have Monique talk about the importance of private health insurance when you are outside your home province or territory, and then we'll have a few minutes at the end of the meeting for questions," said Terry.

CHAPTER 14

Medical Insurance

Policy Choices and Limitations

"Monique works with a company that offers private health-care coverage amongst other insurance products; this is an important consideration that you should look at before spending time in the U.S.," Terry continued. "Coincidentally, I ran into Monique while running errands yesterday at the mall. We have known each other for about 10 years; Monique personally handles my family's supplementary health insurance plans." Terry nodded to Monique to begin.

"Thank you, Terry. I am pleased to be here today to present you with information on private out-of-province or -territory health insurance information," said Monique.

"Health insurance plans and coverage in Canada are different from that in the U.S. Are you aware that your provincial or territorial health insurance plan may not cover much, if any, of the cost of U.S. health and medical care? It is important that you supplement your provincial or territorial health plan with out-of-province coverage. The last thing you want to worry about is becoming ill while you are enjoying your time in the U.S.; however, accidents and illness can occur unexpectedly and at anytime and anywhere. You want to be covered and have access to quality health care.

"The U.S. health-care system is also quite different from Canada's. If you require medical care, a hospital stay, or medication while in the U.S., there could be significant expenses related to obtaining health and medical facility care. Your provincial or territorial plan may cover only a small portion of these costs—or perhaps none of it—while you are in the U.S., and potentially leave you personally responsible for any services and other expenses not provided for by the plan. Some hospitals in the U.S. may not even admit patients lacking medical coverage of some kind. Not having medical coverage is risky. And most provinces and territories have limits on the amounts they will pay for Canadians needing health care in the U.S., or in any foreign country for that matter.

"Health-care plans may also limit the length of time you can be outside your province or territory and still be eligible to receive coverage. Most provinces and territories mandate that as long as your primary residence remains in that specific province or territory, you are generally allowed to be away from your home province or territory for a predetermined number of days before you lose your residency status and your provincial or territorial health-care coverage. For example, Ontario allows an Ontario resident to be away up to 212 days in a predetermined 12-month period. Exceptions may apply for longer out-of-province stays for various reasons—but, and this is important, they must be approved before your departure. It is important for you to be aware of your home province or territory health-care rules, coverage limits, and absence timeframes; you do not want to lose access to your provincial or territorial health insurance program. It is a good idea to check with your province or territory for specific details," explained Monique.

Michelle commented, "I agree, this really is an important item to consider—I had to make private health insurance arrangements for Isabella, who is attending school in the U.S., and I was surprised at the potential cost—and risk—if a health issue or accident occurred and she required medical attention or hospitalization while she was out of province. I also found that there were a number of different insurers, each with different coverage, limitations, exclusions, and pricing."

Coverage Limitations and Deductibles

"It is prudent to purchase additional medical coverage, and there are several out-of-country plans to choose from: plans vary not only in price but also in coverage," Monique continued. "A medical emergency such as a heart attack or car accident could drive up medical and hospital expenses into the thousands, or even tens of thousands, of dollars or more. Depending on the medical condition being treated and the facility, an overnight stay in a U.S. hospital could cost several thousand dollars. Additionally, consider potential costs for ambulance service, prescriptions, transportation, accommodation— they can add up. Many people don't realize how expensive medical and hospital expenses can be in the U.S. Having medical and hospital insurance and coverage is important for both short trips to the U.S. and longer stays. Buying the cheapest policy may provide you with inadequate coverage; be sure to understand what is covered and any exclusions. And get everything in writing. Evaluate your options, coverage, and the price. Make sure you understand the rules. Read the fine print and know what is covered and what's not, before you travel.

"Rates can vary depending on the insurer. Ideally, you want a policy that covers all the expenses that your province does with no limitation on fees or hospital costs. You will need to consider limitation amounts to your coverage, whether it be $1 million, $2 million, $5 million, or even $10 million, or perhaps, although difficult to find, no limitation at all. Compare the cost and coverage differences between a $2-million and $5-million policy, say—you may be surprised that the cost difference is minimal. That being the case, and all other things being equal, consider that you will likely have greater peace of mind with the higher coverage. Like any kind of insurance, a deductible may apply, ranging from $100 to $5,000 or possibly more. Ask if the deductible is payable on a per claim or per policy basis. Often, taking a higher deductible can reduce the premium. In addition to medical treatment, hospitalization, and prescriptions, to name a few items, ask if the policy includes living expenses for your spouse and/or family and return airfare to your home once you are able to travel.

"Find out the insurer's definition of a 'pre-existing condition'— if pre-existing medical conditions are included and, if not, what are the limitations and timeframes. Proceed with caution: ask the insurer for its specific definition of what it considers a stable pre-existing condition, and if you qualify. Be very specific—remember, insurance companies' definitions of pre-existing conditions and what they very specifically define as being stable may be unique to each. Be careful about not reporting a pre-existing condition, even if you have already purchased a policy. Be sure that you understand the pre-existing condition section and clauses of your policy—find out if any pre-existing condition applies before your departure date, rather than when you purchased the policy. This could make a big difference, especially if you have an annual plan. Be honest; a nonreported, pre-existing condition may not be covered, and you would be responsible for the expense. Ask, be specific to your individual circumstances, and read and understand the policy wording before you leave your home province or territory. Get it in writing.

"Some policies may have age restrictions or age-related rates depending on the length of time of coverage. Remember to include your children on your out-of-province medical insurance policies. Similar to here at home, children can be prone to accidents—they may catch the flu, or have a fever or other illness requiring medical attention. Many policies have maximum timeframes that you are able to be away from your home province. These time frames range from a few weeks to six months. Often extensions are available for a fee.

"In addition, some insurers have a toll-free 24-hour/ seven-days-a-week telephone number to call for assistance in an emergency. If a medical emergency or illness occurs while you are away, your insurer may instruct that you or someone close to you call this 24/7 number immediately. In some cases, the insurance emergency call centre will coordinate with the medical facility or hospital to make sure that your treatment is covered. You may be issued a small pocket or wallet card with your policy; the medical facility or hospital may ask for this. Ask if the insurer will accept direct billing from the medical facility. Sometimes and depending on the situation, you may be required to pay for the service—say, at a small clinic—and then submit your receipts to the insurer to be reimbursed. Find out in advance how a claim will be handled," Monique suggested.

"Monique, can you advise whom we can speak with or where we can go to obtain out-of-country health insurance? The only experience I have is with travel agents when I've booked weekly holidays and they offer travel and health insurance as a package," said Michelle.

Health Questionnaire and Pre-Existing Conditions

"You could research insurance plans that are available through insurance companies, automobile clubs, credit cards, some major Canadian banks, insurance brokers, and travel agencies. Cost is usually based on age. If you are older than age 55, usually you will need to answer a detailed medical or health questionnaire before receiving a quote or price for coverage. It is important that you complete the medical questionnaire honestly and accurately, and if you don't understand a question or are unsure how to answer the questions, you might request that your family doctor help complete the questionnaire. As previously emphasized, if you are unsure if a pre-existing condition is covered, call the insurer and ask for a specific explanation of the coverage in the policy and, ideally, get the explanation in writing. Don't leave anything to chance.

"It is also a good idea to find out from the insurer whether the policy covers the cost of returning to your home province or territory for further treatment for yourself or family members traveling with you. Find out whether you will be required to pay for medical expenses yourself and then recover the expenses from the insurer or whether the insurer compensates the physician, medical facility, or hospital directly. In addition, ask the insurer whether you need to get approval from the insurance company before receiving medical treatment," said Monique.

Read the Fine Print: Credit Cards

"I think my credit card provides medical coverage, as well as coverage if I rent a car. Would I need a supplementary insurance policy?" asked Rob.

"Find out from your credit card company exactly what is covered; ask if it is limited medical coverage, and if so, specifically what for and if there are any age or other restrictions. In addition to what is covered, and limitations and deductibles, find out if there is a time limit on the coverage. If you have multiple insurance coverage, it is also wise to find out how any claim should be handled, as well as if it affects future coverage and in what way. It is always best to investigate specifically what is included, what limitations may exist, any deductibles, and, of course, the amount of time you can spend out of country and province or territory and still have coverage.

"Be careful about your credit card covering a rental car; some credit cards may provide collision damage coverage, but they often don't cover liability, theft, or loss of use for the rental company if the car is unrentable while being repaired. Third-party liability is important—this protects you for damages done to others. Make sure you are covered, both in Canada and the U.S., and for that matter anywhere else in the world.

"Some insurers offer a single-trip policy, or an annual coverage policy that covers you for multiple trips over the course of a 12-month period. Multiple-trip medical plans usually have coverage for a specific numbers of days, such as one week, or 21 days, or perhaps even three months. Find out the terms and conditions of each type of policy, as well as the number of days in one stretch that you are allowed to be away from your home province or territory. You may find an insurer that offers additional features, such as a trip cancellation or interruption, and baggage loss or delay. Keep in mind that policies differ. Don't assume that the coverage in one insurer's policy is the same as another insurer's policy. Find out in advance what is included and excluded, for what length of time, what the limitations and deductibles are, and at what cost. Most insurance policies have conditions and exclusions. Do your homework," said Monique.

"While we are talking about insurance, before spending time in the U.S. it is prudent to confirm that your Canadian home insurance policy has freezing peril and snow-loading clauses. Most policies state that when you are away, the home must be checked regularly—ask your insurance company for its definition of 'regularly.' For example, some home insurance policies state that your home needs to be checked daily, or every few days. Find out before departing what the rules are and be sure to note any exclusions.

"If you are driving your Canadian vehicle to the U.S., contact your automobile insurer to find out if there are any limitations or restrictions on your auto coverage while you are out of Canada. For example, if you are driving your vehicle to the U.S. and you plan to view investment property, your insurer may rate the vehicle under a different category. Find this out before departing. Check with both the state and county you plan to drive to as well; if you have an extended stay, find out if the state or county has any licensing rules or requirements. You want to ensure that you are complying with the laws, as well as confirm that you have appropriate and adequate insurance coverage. Do this prior to departing.

"I want to emphasize the importance of doing your homework before traveling outside your province. Proper insurance coverage reduces financial risk and will provide peace of mind. And remember that charges for medical procedures and other medical-related expenses in the U.S. are often more expensive than is the case in Canada," Monique cautioned.

Terry stood up. "Well, thank you very much, ladies!" she said. "On behalf of the group, we are most grateful to you both for sharing your time and this important information with us." Patricia and Monique smiled and nodded to the group.

"I would be happy to stay for a few minutes after the meeting today if anyone has any questions," said Patricia.

It is important that you arrange private health insurance coverage for any trip outside your province or territory. Make sure you know the rules—what is covered and what is not, conditions, exceptions, maximum limits, and deductibles, amongst other items. The options and items reviewed in this chapter are for information purposes only. Seek professional assistance for your individual and family needs.

"Wonderful, and thank you, Patricia," Terry said. "We have covered a great deal these last few weeks. If you recall from our first meeting, determining your goals and budget and getting preapproved for financing, if necessary, is the first step. Once this is completed, decide on the city and state you wish to buy your property in, and determine your needs and wants—your Buyer Property Profile. It is also wise to consult with cross-border professionals to discuss estate and tax issues, and other rules and laws."

Helen stood up. "Terry, this is fantastic. I can't wait to get started."

"Yes, I agree," said Michelle. "Terry, this makes all the difference in my buying experience. I just feel very comfortable and confident."

"I'm glad that you have found the program helpful. I'm excited for all of you," Terry replied.

CHAPTER 15

Renting Your Property

What You Need to Know about Property Management

While Cathy and Rob made the trip to Orlando, Florida, Laura and Marty visited Naples, Florida, and purchased a condo, which they planned to rent out long term. Their strategy was somewhat different from Cathy and Rob's: Marty's parents owned a condo in the same building where they made their purchase. As they were 20 years away from retiring, Laura and Marty wanted to build a portfolio of income-producing properties, with a goal of paying off the mortgages over the next five to 10 years. With three to five income-producing properties paid off, they might then choose to sell some or all of them and purchase their own family property when they were closer to retiring and able to spend more time in Florida.

Because of the decline in real estate prices and current rental rates, factoring in anticipated expenses, Marty and Laura felt the properties would provide neutral to positive cash flow. They knew they could stay in Marty's parents' condo whenever they needed to make a trip to Florida to deal with the property.

Cathy contacted Laura to see if her son, Tim, needed to be dropped off. She said, "I heard through the grapevine that you and Marty bought a condo in south Florida."

"Word travels quickly. Yes, we did. How did you hear?" asked Laura.

"The boys, of course. Did your son tell you our news?"

"What news? Did you and Rob find something?"

"Yes, we did. We just closed."

"Congratulations. That's great! I'm thrilled for you both. With our condo, we plan on renting it out as an investment, so it is a little different from buying a vacation property."

"Do you have renters yet?"

"Not yet. We're working with a property management company to find renters," replied Laura.

"Are you planning to rent the condo to the same people all year, or are you considering short-term or seasonal renters?"

"For convenience, we ideally want to rent it on an annual basis; however, we are told that we would likely net more rental income if we were willing to rent for shorter-term timeframes. We don't want to have to furnish and outfit the condo for short-term renters, and we don't want to bother dealing with arranging for keys and cleaning, and so on. The condo has a minimum timeframe that we can rent on a short-term basis," replied Laura.

"What services are your property manager undertaking—things like collecting rent each month, handling the maintenance, and paying the bills?"

"Let's see," said Laura. "I have a list—our property manager has these responsibilities:

- Acting as first point of contact for tenants and maintenance personnel
- Advertising and marketing the property to find suitable tenants
- Screening prospective tenants, including doing a credit check and employment verification
- Looking after the lease contract and paperwork
- Collecting the monthly rent from tenants

- Ensuring that tenants are happy and carrying out their tenant responsibilities
- Managing interior and exterior maintenance and repair
- Doing general banking and other administrative responsibilities, such as reporting and record retention

"Marty and I don't have the time to do it ourselves, and we want a professional to handle it for us," said Laura.

"How did you find your property manager?" asked Cathy.

"Marty's parents recommended her; she was their property manager when they used to rent out their condo."

"Ah, recommendations are usually the best source."

"Before we hired our property manager, on the advice of our real estate broker we had browsed through the website (www.irem.org) of the Institute of Real Estate Management. We reviewed the owner/investor section. We also looked at the website www.narpm.org, which is the National Association of Real Property Managers. Both websites provided a lot of information," said Laura.

"Thanks for the tip. I think I will call Nina, my real estate broker, and ask her what she thinks as well," said Cathy. "Oh, we'll drop Tim off in about an hour if that works."

"That's fine. It was great talking to you, and congratulations on your new condo. Some day we may run into one another at the airport or in Florida! See you at the hockey banquet next week."

* * *

"Hi, Nina. You thought you would be rid of us once we bought and closed on our house, but I have yet another question!" said Cathy.

"You know I always enjoy hearing from you. What's on your mind?" Nina said, laughing.

"I was speaking with a friend today, who told me that she and her husband purchased a condo that they plan to rent out. They are using a property manager that his family has used in the past to assist them with this. Although Rob and I purchased our property for our families to use, we are considering renting it part time if it is feasible. We are also thinking about purchasing over this next year or two a couple of investment properties to rent out long term, so I wanted to get some information on how to find a property manager. Do you have any tips on how we can find a good property manager?" asked Cathy.

"It's important that you differentiate between a property manager and a real estate professional who does some property management," Nina replied. "Ideally, you will want to hire a professional who specializes in property management. There are property management companies that specialize solely in property management. You should interview a few potential property managers, find out the services they provide and at what cost, and ask for and check references before hiring her or him. The management of properties should be done in an efficient and economical manner. A property manager is an important member of your investment team; it is important that you spend the time to find a good fit."

Interview Questions for a Property Manager

"When interviewing potential property managers, you might want to consider asking these questions," Nina said, and proceeded to read from her list:

1. *How many properties do you currently have under management?* Volume can be an asset—find out how much experience the manager has and the number of years in business. Also ask how many owners he or she manages for. Ideally, you want a property manager who manages several properties with various owners.

2. *What is your company's ratio of vacancies to the total number of properties it manages?* Compare the vacancy ratio to that of the overall market.

3. *Do you manage any properties in the same area as my property? If yes, how many? Where is the property management office located?* Proximity to the property is very important.

4. *What type of property do you manage in my area?* For example, if you are purchasing a first-time starter house with an average size of 1,200 square feet, find out if the property manager has other similar houses in the area under management. This means he or she works with a similar tenant base.

5. *What do you do to ensure that a property is always rented? How do you find tenants?* Ask about how the company markets your property for rent—what types of advertising and signage, and if it has a website. Ask how it is different from its competition.

6. *What are your rent collection procedures? When and how do you collect the rent?* This is an important part of the property management task.

7. *How will I receive my money each month from rental income?* Ask if the property management company has auto direct deposit into your bank account. Ask what date the deposit is made each month.

8. *What do you do if the tenant doesn't pay the rent?* Find out what the state or county laws are regarding nonpayment of rent.

9. *What are the state and county eviction rules? What are your eviction procedures?* Experienced property management companies have a system for rent collection and evictions.

10. *Does the company own any investment property? If so, in what community?*

11. *What are your fees? Do you charge a placement fee? How are the fees billed and paid?* Typically, management fees range from 8 to 14 per cent, depending on the area and property. Short-term rental fees may vary between 30 and 50 per cent of the weekly rental amount in some areas. Fees vary depending on the state and county. Do your own research—find out

what is reasonable in your chosen area. Ask what is included in the fee—what the property management company does. Often property management companies charge an up-front placement fee for finding the tenant; then they charge a percentage of collected rent. Ask what happens if the rent isn't collected—does the company still expect to collect its fee, and if so, why?

12. *Are there any extra fees? What are they?*

13. *What reports do you prepare and when are they sent out? Are they e-mailed or mailed to you each month?* You should expect to receive a statement every month outlining the rent collected, expenses, and the balance remitted to the owner. Regular communication with your property manager is important.

14. *Do you pay housing-related bills—for example, HOA fees and property tax—and deduct the expense from the monthly rental income?*

15. *Does the property management company handle maintenance and repairs in-house?* Ask if there is a policy for repairs up to a predefined amount. For example, any repair over $100 requires written permission from the owner.

16. *Do you have a team of contractors and/or other maintenance professionals to whom you subcontract work?* Find out if the property management company marks up the subcontractors' invoices.

17. *Does the property manager obtain three bids or quotes for any repairs or required improvements? Will I be sent the bids to review and approve?*

18. *Will you provide a few client references that I may contact?*

19. *Will you provide a copy of a management agreement in advance for my review?*

"Do your research and interview the property managers," Nina summed up. "Ongoing good property management for investment properties is very important. If you are planning to acquire investment properties in the U.S., remember that you live in a different country, and quite a distance from the property. A property manager is local—he or she lives in the city where your investment property is located. This is important, as the property manager should be doing regular property checks, has relationships with local tradespeople and maintenance staff, deals with the tenant directly, and is knowledgeable about the local rental market. Typically, you get what you pay for.

"You will need to inquire specifically about short-term rentals; usually the fees are higher. Find out what services will be provided and at what cost," said Nina.

"A friend gave me the websites of property management associations: the National Association of Real Property Managers and the Institute of Real Estate Management. I am beginning to research for a property manager," said Cathy.

"That sounds like a good starting point. And I can give you the names of several property management companies for you to also research and interview. Also ask around—you may be surprised what you find. It is also a good idea to ask the potential property managers for the contact information for a couple of current and past customers so that you can get feedback on their service," suggested Nina.

"It is very important to confirm specifically what the property manager's responsibilities are each month and what the cost is. It is a good idea to get this in writing. Also check with your homeowners association or condo regarding short-term rentals—make sure you are able to rent short term. Get the rules or regulations in writing. Some states or counties may also charge a tourist tax for short-term rentals. You might want to check with either the county in which your property is located or an accountant who is familiar with state law.

"It is also important that you spend the time searching for and interviewing property management companies and understand the rules. In the long run, it's worth the time spent," said Nina.

"I guess if we decide to rent out the property part time we will need to file U.S. as well as Canadian tax returns. There should not be much, if any, tax to pay, but I remember what the accountant said about complying with the tax rules. Perhaps I'll call her and find out if there is a tourist tax for short-term rentals in Florida, and discuss our goals in terms of acquiring investment property," said Cathy.

"Smart idea," responded Nina. "Sounds like you have a lot of work to do."

CONSIDERATIONS WHEN HIRING A PROPERTY MANAGER

1. **Property management agreement**—Determine and understand the responsibilities of the property manager as well as the costs. Costs vary—they can range between 8 and 14 per cent of the monthly lease amount depending on the property, the marketplace, and the agreed-upon work, and often there may be a placement fee. Some firms charge flat rates or "à la carte" fees for specific services. For short-term rentals, the fees are negotiable but are typically higher.

2. **References**—Ask for referrals of past and current customers and be sure to call and speak with these customers. You want to ascertain the quality of service and attention that you will likely get from the property management company.

3. **Location of company**—It is important that you select a property manager located near your property. You want a property manager that is attentive to your property and makes the routine site inspections. Reflect before you hire a property manager that is a long drive from the property— you may find that the property does not receive the attention it deserves.

4. **Contractor pricing**—Property managers normally have a list of contractors that they routinely work with. Occasionally, when a medium to larger task is being completed, consider calling to get your own quote from an independent contractor (e.g., for plumbing, furnace, or pool service). This will help ensure you are getting a competitive price.

5. **Agreement timeframe**—Be careful about signing or agreeing to a property management agreement for longer than
   one year. Often, when you sign the original lease contract,
   you are agreeing to pay the property management fees for
   the duration of the lease—even if it is two or three years, or
   longer. The problem is if you decide to discontinue using the
   property management company: it may be entitled to continue to collect all the remaining monthly fees. Sign a one-
   year property management agreement and review the level
   of service at year-end. It is also wise to have your attorney
   write the lease.

EPILOGUE

During the next four months, six couples purchased U.S. property. Cathy and Rob, Helen and Jay, and Eliza and Roger purchased vacation property in Florida. Laura and Marty purchased an investment condo in Naples, have just finalized a rental agreement with their tenants, and have a plan to acquire another investment property within the year. Michelle and David purchased a vacation house in Arizona in joint ownership with friends; Mary and J.P. purchased a vacation property in Palm Springs, California. Two couples purchased their vacation property for personal use and are going to try to offset their maintenance and carrying costs by renting the property short term; three couples purchased solely for personal use, and one couple purchased as an investment property. Lindsey has completed the preapproval process and begun searching for an investment property in the Miami area.

APPENDIX

Executing Your Purchase Plan

Each year, hundreds of thousands of Canadians visit the U.S. For many Canadians, a warmer climate away from the chilly and snowy Canadian winter months is attractive—both as a retirement lifestyle vehicle and as an investment. Owning real estate in the U.S. has become a dream come true for many Canadians. And it can be for you as well. Here's how to get started.

The first step is to set up a consultation to discuss your personal buyer program. At the outset, your budget (and mortgage financing where applicable), geographical preferences, and wants and needs—in other words, your Buyer Property Profile—will be reviewed. Then you will have the opportunity to set up appointments to meet with cross-border legal and tax professionals to discuss your individual needs and goals. Consideration should be given to estate planning, titling, and potential tax responsibilities, to name a few.

A detailed outline of all anticipated costs, closing fees, and down payment requirements related to your U.S. real estate purchase will be covered by these independent professionals. There should be no surprises.

And remember, you are not alone. I have access to a network of experienced U.S. real estate brokers. Collectively this team of professionals works together to systematically guide, educate, and assist you—a complete advisory package for the Canadian buyer of U.S. real estate.

A website has been created for your reference. Please go to www.RealEstateKim.com, where you will find updates, articles, important property buying information, mortgage calculators and other helpful tools. Register for an upcoming U.S. buying seminar.

It is important for you to have a team of experienced professionals. While it is an undertaking you may manage yourself, it may be worth considering the alternative of having a network of experienced real estate, legal, tax, and mortgage professionals who are willing to assist and guide you through this exciting process.

If you would like to get started via e-mail, go to RealEstateKim.com and, from under the Let's Get Started tab, download the Introductory Summary. Fill in the form and send it back, and we will contact you.

Every day you delay is a day your dream to own U.S. real estate is deferred. As said during the Blackhawks championship-game pep talk—it's your time to score!

Note: www.RealEstateKim.com is managed by Kimberley Marr, Broker, ABR®, CAAP, IRES, RE/MAX® Professionals Inc., Brokerages. (905) 270-8840

ACKNOWLEDGEMENTS

This book reflects the experience and skills of several professionals who collectively contributed their time in answering questions and providing in-depth knowledge during the research and writing process. I am grateful to these professionals who generously shared their time, knowledge, resources, and enthusiasm for the book—it was truly a team effort.

Special thanks to Pamela Alexander, CEO RE/MAX® Integra Corporation, who embraced the book and program whole-heartedly. Your support and encouragement, for the manuscript, in addition to the passion you have for the real estate profession as well as serving the public is never-ending. We are all fortunate to have you as a mentor, visionary and leader—both at the professional and consumer level. Thank you, Pamela.

In alphabetical order, I am grateful to the following professionals who spent hours answering questions, reading the manuscript, and providing information and feedback on their areas of expertise, including David A. Altro, Florida attorney, Canadian legal counsel, author of *Owning U.S. Property - The Canadian Way*, Managing Partner, Altro & Associates,

LLP; Susan Inez Poskus, President, Thomas C. Roberge & Company; Jeffery Rolke, TD Waterhouse; and Barbara Vance, RE/MAX® Properties Southwest.

In each case, your enthusiasm, contribution of professional knowledge, and support for this manuscript is greatly appreciated. This book would not be what it is without all of your collective input and support.

To my colleague Christine Mitchell, Broker/Manager, RE/MAX® Professionals Inc.: I remember that cool but sunny day when we first spoke about the book; you didn't skip a beat. Your support, encouragement and big-picture thinking are greatly appreciated.

Christine Martysiewicz, Director Internal & Public Relations, RE/MAX® Ontario Atlantic Canada: I value your comments, ideas and professional guidance. Thank you for your resources and the time you have spent on the project. I am fortunate to work with such a supportive and knowledgeable team.

Linda Sansom, General Manager, RE/MAX® Professionals Inc.: there are no coincidences in life. I thank you for being there to bounce ideas off. I am grateful for the time you have spent researching rules, practices, and sharing your professional resources.

I would like to thank Don Loney, Executive Editor, John Wiley & Sons Canada, Ltd., for continuous encouragement and dedication to the book. I appreciate you patiently answering my many questions and for your ongoing assistance. I am also thankful for the support and assistance of the entire Wiley team—you are all a pleasure to work with.

On a personal note, I wish to acknowledge and thank my family and friends. I feel blessed to share a special place in your lives and look forward to many future memories.

ABOUT THE AUTHOR

Kimberley Marr, CAAP, ABR®, IRES member, a 23-year-veteran real estate broker with RE/MAX® Professionals, Inc., focuses her career on helping buyers and sellers achieve their real estate investment goals and dreams. She is the author of two books, *Your First Home: A Buyer's Kit - For Condos and Houses!* (Self-Counsel Press) and *How To Buy U.S. Real Estate with The Personal Property Purchase System* (John Wiley & Sons). Whether she is representing first-time home buyers, or working with luxury, condominium, waterfront, investment, or international buyers or sellers, Kim's objective-oriented and systematic approach begins by educating buyers and sellers on the many factors involved in their real estate process. Kim believes that prudent decisions should be made based on understanding the available options and having access to reliable resources, and so avoiding unwanted surprises. Her philosophy is to put the client's needs first and always strive for optimal results. This has been a driving force behind her successful real estate career and has earned her numerous prestigious awards.

Over the last 17 years, Kim has instructed and presented a variety of programs at a number of continuing education, university and industry venues. She has been a speaker and panelist at national and international real estate, mortgage and industry-related conferences, made television as well as radio appearances, and been interviewed by local newspaper as well as real estate related publications. Her energetic and engaging presentation style entertains as well as informs audiences, yet also provides a realistic and planned approach or system for defining and executing your real estate goals.

Kim has an active role in the real estate industry and community. She is a past director on the local real estate board, is an active member of CREA, OREA, TREB, MREB, REBAC, and IRES. Charities and causes that Kim supports include Children's Miracle Network, and Breast Cancer. A portion of the proceeds from the book will be donated to these charities.

INDEX